DON'T TELL ANYONE

Don't Tell Anyone

My Adoption Journey from Secrets & Lies to Discovery & Understanding

MICHAEL F. LUCK

Rand-Smith Books

Copyright © 2024 by Michael F. Luck

Paperback: 978-1-959544-49-3
Digital/Ebook: 978-1-950544-50-9

All rights reserved. No part of this book may be reproduced in any manner whatsoever without written permission except in the case of brief quotations embodied in critical articles and reviews.

Photos from the author's personal collection.

Rand-Smith Publishing
Printed in the USA

First Printing, 2024

DEDICATION

To my three children with love:

Sean Michael Luck
Holly Marie Luck
Jonathan Wilson Luck

and my grandchildren
Patrick Ryan Luck
Kathryn Rachel Luck

CONTENTS

DEDICATION - v
ACKNOWLEDGMENTS - xi
PREAMBLE - xiv

A Time of Innocence

~ 1 ~
A Different Prism
2

~ 2 ~
A Luck-y Life
5

~ 3 ~
Young, Foolish, and Forgiven
21

~ 4 ~
A Nomadic Life
32

~ 5 ~
The Uninvited Apparition
42

Time Heals All Wounds

~ 6 ~

Information Overload

52

~ 7 ~

The Conversation

60

~ 8 ~

Full Circle

71

The Mystery of Love

~ 9 ~

High Expectations

78

~ 10 ~

A Plan of Convenience

85

~ 11 ~

Closed and Confidential

92

Prying Open the Last Secret

~ 12 ~

The Extra Son

98

~ 13 ~
For Those Living Alone
109

~ 14 ~
"This Is My Son"
120

~ 15 ~
The Layers Unfold
129

~ 16 ~
Another Door Opens
136

A New Beginning

~ 17 ~
The Fifth Son
146

~ 18 ~
Wardian Acceptance
161

~ 19 ~
The Rudderless Ship
169

~ 20 ~
Cheated by Death
176

~ 21 ~

The Man in the Wind

184

~ 22 ~

The Fifth Avenue Girl

191

Epilogue

198

ABOUT THE AUTHOR - 203

ACKNOWLEDGMENTS

This book began as an effort to "tell myself my own story" by writing it down so I might believe it. I wished to discover the truth of my adoption and to share it with my immediate family and generations to come. Everyone seemed to know parts of the story and details were fuzzy. It took several years of collecting and drawing upon source documents before I began the arduous process of writing. The driving force was to faithfully capture the whole story in one place.

It is with deep gratitude I recognize those who accompanied me on this journey. So many provided exceptional coaching and reflection and shared personal sentiments, which informed and affirmed the story.

Without Beth Thomas, an adoption search specialist, there would be no story.

I express to her my great, heartfelt appreciation for all of her gracious, professional, and kind assistance in finding both of my biological parents.

From the onset of the search for my biological parents, my wife, Barbara Wilson, encouraged me. She shared a fascination for uncovering the adoption story and forging new family relationships. I am extremely grateful for her devoted partnership, reading, adding, and editing many drafts over several years, without which this story may not have been told.

Editor David Smitherman completed my story. His superb writing mastery kept me focused clearly on the adoption narrative when my emotions interfered. His suggestions, deletions, and additions were just perfect. He bestowed upon me his special gift – the craft of storytelling. To him, I extend my sincerest gratitude.

Dear friend Diane Nine, a seasoned speaker's bureau and book agent, provided monumental advice. When I asked, "how and where I might self-publish 50 copies for my family, relatives, and friends," she recognized the value of my story and graciously shared the manuscript with several publishers. She is the champion catalyst that made this book possible and I will be forever grateful.

I acknowledge with sincere thanks Rand-Smith Publishing Company for accepting for publication and graciously working with me to put everything in good order. The publishers were amazing and dedicated, which was a thrill. For that, I am especially grateful and express my warm appreciation.

Special recognition goes to two published authors.

Jones Deady, a good friend and author of *The Steep Side of the Marble* (2020 Rand-Smith Publishers), read the very early drafts of this manuscript and made helpful suggestions. Terence Ward, my half- brother and author of several books (www.terenceward.com), provided helpful and constructive suggestions. I fondly remember reciting early chapter drafts to him as we rode across the country on a family mission.

Most importantly, my biological and adoptive family members deserve special recognition. Each has a role in the story. Many provided family letters, videos, musings, and personal accounts: Cousin Nancy Titus shared her father, James Ward's, writings about early family life in Donegal, Ireland, and Bayonne, New Jersey; John (Sean) Ward's wife, Flo provided videos of historic family gatherings as well as my birth father and mother, four half-others and cousins. All these contributions are reflected in the story.

My cousins, the Leddy family, especially John and Jimmy, as well as Ann Leddy Charron, shared details of my adoptive mother Mary Luck's family history uncovered in their family archives. I am forever indebted to each for their kind support all my life.

Adoptive Parents
William H. and Mary A. (Leddy) Luck
and
Birth Parents
Patrick J. Ward and Rita June (Boomhower) Mills

Sisters
Nancy Jane Luck Edwards
Rosemary Ann Luck

Wife
Barbara C. Wilson

Former Spouse
Barbara Lee Benzie

Half-Brothers
Kevin Ward
Terence Ward
Christopher Ward
Richard Ward

PREAMBLE

Don't Tell Anyone is not the whole story. It never could be. There's too much to tell. A second book could be written just about my family, relatives, friends, and colleagues. Nevertheless, it is a true story, or at least as true as it can be. While everyone creates their own truth, it never grows in a straight line. It's always full of twists and turns. The "twists" are secrets, and the "turns" are choices made.

This is a story about confession, contrition, and forgiveness, a compilation of memory, important source documents, and reflection over more than seven decades. It is a narrative to describe personal provenance discovered from the collective impact of unexpected pregnancies, profound choices, and altered life trajectories. It threads the highlights of birth parents, adoptive parents, personal family, and the process of making sense of all the pieces. Who are we really, where are we going, and how did we get here?

Most importantly, this story is about secrets that represent hope, discovery, and the search for some wild and original truth to appear. Some parts are recreated to serve as lessons, while others are absolute truths etched into memory.

In this story, honesty and heartache stare back with uncomfortable intensity. It is a forlorn, aching tale that twins on Irish fable and hard reality.

We all hold our own truths.

These are mine.

A Time of Innocence

~ 1 ~

A DIFFERENT PRISM

In 1962, the Beatles had just conducted an unsuccessful audition in the U.S. with Decca Records and were told "guitar groups were on the way out," and a Catholic Bishop in Buffalo announced that Chubby Checker's song, "The Twist" would be banned from all Catholic schools because it was impure.

I was fifteen.

My friends and I frequented Henry's Diner in downtown Burlington, Vermont. It was our favorite after-school meeting place. Together, we crammed into a red vinyl corner booth. Our food orders were always identical: Coke, French fries, and gravy.

In the midst of jokes and conversation during one of our meetings, I mindlessly rummaged through my bookbag for a pencil, and the family Bible fell out. I had it that day at school for a special religion class. After picking it up, I noticed several blank white pages. They were new to me. Some of the pages contained handwritten descriptions of births, deaths, marriages, and other important family milestones on each page. I was fascinated with all the entries depicting vital statistics of our family: the comings and goings of grandmothers, grandfathers, aunts, and uncles.

Then, the last entry took my breath away. It read:

Michael Frederick Luck,

Born March 26, 1947

Adopted June 16, 1949

There was my name clear as day, followed by the word "adopted." I stared for what felt like an eternity, my thoughts swirling to make sense of it all. There must have been some mistake. Perhaps, *adopted* was another word for "baptism" at church. I was unsure what to say or do.

"Earth to Michael," one of my buddies said with a laugh.

I looked up and asked, "What does *adopt* mean?" The uncomfortable silence was palpable. To break the tension, I muttered, "Oh, forget it, I'm kidding. I know what it means."

The guys picked up on their original conversations as if nothing had happened, but I was left reeling.

For the remainder of the day, I couldn't focus on anything else. Could I really be adopted? My mind raced. Was my little sister, Rosemary, also adopted? I vaguely remember my mother not being pregnant with her, but I was only five, and the details are hazy. What about my older sister, Nancy? Was she adopted as well? If so, did my sisters and I come from the same parents?

My immediate thought was that if I was adopted, my parents simply must have forgotten to tell me. They certainly wouldn't have kept such important information to themselves. Maybe they had planned on having the talk once I got older, and life just got in the way. Seemed perfectly logical. I couldn't imagine such an important omission being intentional. However, back then, adoptions were quiet, secretive affairs, kept under wraps with admonitions of "don't tell anyone." That was considered the best way to protect everyone in "the family."

If my assumption was true, I was in fact adopted, that meant the parents I'd grown up loving, trusting, and obeying (most of the time) were not related to me. It seemed unfathomable. Maybe my sisters were not blood relatives either. Then, the larger question remained unanswered. Who was my "real" mother and father, and why had they given me away?

Walking home on that fateful day, I struggled to process my emotions. What clues had I missed over the past fifteen years? Should I now confront my mother and father with the Bible and ask what the entry meant? What would be the purpose? Would there be an ideal time or place to do this? What would be their reaction to the question? Would they be hurt? Angry? What would happen if they thought I already knew? Maybe Nancy knew but had never felt the need to mention it. It was clear that I had many more questions than answers.

Despite all the reservations, I was as sure as a boy could be my parents loved and supported me. I already had proof. Although the Luck household wasn't one of demonstrative hugs, kisses, and exclamations of "I love you," I had always felt safe, warm, and secure. My adoptive parents grew up during the Depression and World War II with low-key emotions and a central theme of "sticking together as a family, working hard, and making the best of things."

So, I decided not to mention my discovery to my parents. In fact, I wasn't going to tell anyone. The uneasiness remained, but I simply decided to do my best to block the idea of adoption from my mind. The fact was that I loved my parents, my sister Nancy, and, of course, little Rosemary, who fought a tragic battle with cystic fibrosis.

There was no question that my parents were doing the best they could for all of us, and I didn't want to disrupt our household.

No matter how strong my resolve in that decision, the news of my adoption altered my vision of my parents. Our loving attachment remained strong, but my brain simply began processing our relationship through a different prism. It was impossible for me to "unknow" what I knew, so I did what I felt was the best option.

While I made the conscious decision to put the idea of adoption out of my mind, I couldn't help but look at my parents a bit differently.

~ 2 ~

A LUCK-Y LIFE

My father, Bill Luck, started dating my mother, Mary Leddy, in 1931.

He worked while taking a few courses at nearby St. Michael's College. After what Mary described as "a long courtship," on June 2, 1936, at 8:30 on a Monday morning, Bill and Mary were married. Even by today's standards a marriage on an early weekday might seem odd, but it worked for their schedules.

During the Depression, Bill worked as a waiter at several restaurants and resorts in Vermont and nearby Lake Dunmore, New York. He was smart, amiable, and handsome, with a good sense of humor. He was later offered a steady job as a route delivery salesman for the Burlington-based McKenzie Meat Packing Company. It was a perfect fit for Bill as he continued to refine his customer service skills. Store owners looked forward to his arrival with fresh meat deliveries. Most of his customers looked forward to his visits, where they would catch up and share a laugh or two. Jerry McKenzie, the company owner, became Bill's lifelong friend. After all, Bill's roots in New England ran deep.

Prior to moving to Burlington, Vermont, Bill's parents, Frank A. and Alice B. (Coffey) Luck, had lived a few short years in Fitchburg, Massachusetts, where Bill was born on April 2, 1910. Shortly thereafter, employed by the textile mills, the Luck family moved to

Amsterdam, New York, later to arrive in Burlington, Vermont, where Bill's father leased and operated a small neighborhood gas station, often relying on family members to pitch in to keep the business going. Bill was one of four children. He had two brothers, Carl and Francis, and a younger sister, Mary (Mamie).

As good fortune would have it, the Luck grandparents lived close by. My paternal grandmother, Alice Luck, was a sweet and loving Irish woman. She doted on me during family visits, while Grandpa Frank remained mostly cantankerous. He sometimes drank too much and had a working history that barely held the family together. My father usually joined his brother Carl to ensure their mother was adequately cared for and safe. Unfortunately, I never knew my Irish maternal grandparents, John and Anna Leddy, who had died young.

My father's solid work ethic continued to pay off. In 1942, Bill was offered an opportunity to work for the U.S. Internal Revenue Service. He seized it and was trained to be a revenue agent. The position gave him an opportunity to advance his education and career with the federal government while offering good benefits for his family.

My mother's family history was quite different. Until the age of 11, Mary grew up on a farm in the foothills of Mt. Mansfield until they learned that the U.S. Government was purchasing lots of remote land in the area for military and weapon training. The Leddy's accepted an offer to sell their property and settle in Burlington with their three children, Mary, Frances, and Bernard, so they might receive a better education. Mary was very bright and excelled in school. She always wanted to be an English teacher. At the age of 18, just as she began her university studies, her career plans were set back when her mother died suddenly. As the oldest of the two girls, she assumed the household responsibilities.

Losing their mother was an unexpected shock and tremendous loss for the Leddy family. In support of a grieving father and the needs of her siblings, Mary was expected to hold the family together, perform household chores, and take care of her father, sister Frances, and brother Bernard, all while pursuing her studies at the University of Vermont. Her determination and hard work paid off when she graduated and became the teacher she always wanted to be.

***

Mary and Bill were introduced to each other by a friend, and the two were exchanging letters in no time. It was clear they were fast falling in love. Both demonstrated an envy of other suitors and enjoyed coy exchanges with affection and teasing.

Bill wrote to Mary:

January 23, 1935, 8:30 p.m.
Dear Mary,
I just got back from supper and decided I should keep my promise to write this letter to you. I am exhausted, as usual, so don't expect a long one, although I could write until dawn, if I weren't.

I see you expect to be well and kicking over this weekend. I also presume you intend to go someplace Friday nite? I presume you are wondering how I came to know all this? Can't you guess? Well, it was this way. Madigan came over to the McKenzie Plant this morning and he brought his usual bunch of clothes. He laid them on the meat block while he was looking around. Lo and behold, I spied the "one and only" red dress creation from Paris belonging to the inimitable Mary Leddy. I immediately grabbed Madigan by the throat and when he was within an inch of his life, he managed to gasp he was only going to clean and press the clothes. He said you were safe and sound for all he knew. After he convinced me, I let him up, and well, we had a good laugh together. I told Madigan you were broke and you wouldn't be able to pay him when your clothes were finished. He put across a sad appearing expression and said he wouldn't be able to do the dresses if he couldn't get his cash. I feel sorry for you, too, Mary. All your good optimism, shot, another weekend at home and this time because Madigan refused to extend his credit. (Ha-Ha.)

You know, Mary, I always thought a guy who would write, "Ha-Ha" after his sentence was out of his head or a pansy, but it's fitting in this instance. Do you share my dry humor, eh!? But humor regardless. I miss your letters. I guess you meant what you said when you told me, "No more letters until you write."

Well, Mary Agnes (like it?) I went to the Flynn Theatre last nite and saw the mighty Barnum, a good show. Too bad you weren't here. But I will tell you all about it so don't feel bad. Maybe if you have any money left, we could go Saturday p.m. or would you rather take in the Palais Royale on Washington Street? I don't think Alex or Mattie will be there. I think if you feel good enough, we can go skating soon. It's 10 degrees below zero tonite and getting colder. Fine weather for polar bears and hot-blooded people.

Well, the hour is late, the writing paper is almost used up, it's cold, and I am tired and have to get up at 5:30 a.m. These are five good reasons for saying so long till Saturday.

Bill

It was clear that Mary loved Bill's letters. She found him funny and entertaining because he could always get a rise out of her. She longed for adult companionship after teaching all day and coming home to a rented room at a boarding house in South Hero, twenty miles north of Burlington. It was far from exciting so she had plenty of time to indulge in the art of correspondence. Being an English teacher, she had no trouble keeping up with Bill and matching his flirtatious wordplay.

Thursday p.m.
Dear Bill,
I have begun to miss you so soon, so I thought I would dash off a few lines. I am rather tired and can't write steadily. I have a couple of nuns from St. Anthony's coming here tonight, trying to hire me for a dollar a day. I have told them I would have to have at least $2 a day so they went home to sleep on it. Maybe I will have a job Monday, but not a position.

Gee, I hope you will come home Saturday. I don't know how I'm going to stand the wait. I guess the next time I will have to go whether you are driving the truck or not? It's real love, don't you think?

I finished cleaning the living room today. It was an all-day job. When I clean, I always imagine the way it should look and I make a plan to make the vision come true.

I will send your watch, along with your suit and shirt. Gee, you don't want your tux, do you? You're not planning on stepping out, are you, Bill? I don't want to push you, but I do hope you will be home Saturday. But, if you can't, I will forgive you and miss you all the more.

So, I will close,
Love, Mary

***

When I was a child, my parents purchased one acre of land in Underhill, about a forty-minute drive from their Burlington home, at a location close to the old Leddy farm. It was an area that Mary knew well and very much loved. With our growing family, Bill and Mary decided to use the land to build a modest camp for summer escapes. The camp, once constructed, had an unobstructed view of Vermont's highest peak, Mt. Mansfield. Cars stopped frequently to take photos. The famous Stowe Ski Resort was on the other side of the mountain.

The Luck Camp was a simple design: one large room about 32 X 24 feet, which included two built-in bunk beds with decorative scalloped wood carvings, a fieldstone fireplace, a small corner kitchen with minimal counters and a refrigerator (an insulated box that held a block of ice). Upon our arrival, Dad and I would make trips to a commercial icehouse to buy blocks of ice to keep things cool. When ice wasn't available, we would store things in a shaded spring nearby. I always volunteered for that chore since it meant I could splash around under the hot summer sun. Attached to the main camp was a 6 x 10-foot extension that housed a chemical toilet, washer/dryer, and a small sink. Later, they added a modest screened porch on the other side of the camp for the mountain view, dining area, and even a sleeping cot for me.

Our family stayed at the family camp all summer and almost every weekend in spring and fall. Dad commuted to work for the IRS in Burlington, Monday through Friday. Both family and friends relished an invitation to come to the Luck Camp to get out of the city for the fresh mountain air and enjoy the warm hospitality.

***

Back in the city, our East Avenue neighborhood was adjacent to the Mary Fletcher Hospital and Trinity College and filled with a great, diverse group of Irish Catholic families. French Canadians and Italians rounded out the community. It was a time when neighbors looked out for one another. Reg and Hazel Ash lived two doors away, kept track of everyone, and could talk anyone's ear off. Next door, the elderly Aucherblad sisters spent much of their time working in the best garden on the street. There was the secretive Mr. and Mrs. Rivers, who kept their curtains closed and were rarely seen. My pals were the Lizotte twins; Bobbie and Tony, the Ravelins; Linda and Steve, the Delormes; Paul and Linda, Tony Little, the Mangans; and always a gaggle of others up and down the street, depending on the activities planned for the day.

Rain or shine, our neighborhood was always filled with childhood screams of delight and imagination. A cluster of children would huddle together and barter to determine which game to play. The more vocal kids would try to sell the other on their idea—hopscotch, hide and go seek, cops and robbers. In case of a stalemate, a game of marbles would always break the tie without showing favoritism. The daily goal was achieving majority agreement on what to do. The stragglers plopped down on the dewy grass and awaited the outcome.

My favorite playground was across the street from our house on an expansive grass-covered flat land with a steep hillside. The property belonged to the Mary Fletcher Hospital, which stood on top of the hill. Winter brought snow to the steep hillside, which fortunately flattened just before the road at the bottom. It was perfect for snow sledding, a smooth ride that ended with a hint of danger. Some of the kids brought out their toboggans and metal discs to tame the icy hill. I avoided those discs because they flew down the hill like a rocket ship with no controls. The only way to avoid crashing into a tree or flying onto the main road was to abandon ship and hurl yourself onto the hard ice. Novices paid careful attention to seasoned veterans in hopes of avoiding a total wipeout in front of their friends.

In the summer, the snowy slope was a distant memory, but that didn't stop us. We crafted makeshift toboggans out of cardboard and hurled ourselves down the wet, grassy knoll as often as possible. We would regularly besiege the nearby appliance store in search of sturdy cardboard boxes that once housed appliances like washers and dryers. We had to return weekly for replacements, especially during the rainy season.

I lived in a modest two-story house with white clapboards, green wooden shutters, and a detached single-car garage. At the rear of the garage was a small chicken coop that provided eggs during WWII when food supplies were short. My sister, Nancy, had the daily chore of searching for the chicken treasures in the straw bedding while dodging the hen's protective pecks. Later, I repurposed the coop as my make-believe grocery store. The elevated entrance for the chickens became a store window where neighborhood friends could place pretend grocery orders. Sometimes, I ran the store, and sometimes, others took over, depending upon negotiations. The store products were merely objects found on the ground, like a pine cone, which became a bottle of milk or a loaf of bread. The only limitation to the store's commerce was our collective imagination.

The entrance to my parents' house had a simple portico. The first floor contained a living and dining room with a kitchen, while the second offered three bedrooms and a bath. However, I was less interested in the living space as I found the attic and basement more intriguing. The attic, a secret world, revealed itself through a door and up a set of stairs from one of the bedrooms. I could stand up straight in the middle of the attic, but a slight shift to the right or left and I'd have to crouch to avoid bumping my head. At the far end, I cleared an area of boxes and old trunks to make space for my "mad scientist" laboratory. I had strewn the lab table with collections of nature's curiosities, mysterious experiments, and dissected creatures.

Regularly, I raided the dumpster bins at the Vermont Department of Health and Research located across the street to retrieve discarded glass vials, tubes, and beakers for my laboratory. It never occurred to me that the items being thrown away might be dangerous or contaminated. I just found them intriguing and magical. On especially warm days the attic had an aroma of fermenting alcohol and dead animals. Most of my friends frequently declined my eager invitations to visit, perhaps thinking they might be next.

Like most neighborhoods, all my friends had a cadre of weapons of terror: spitballs, slingshots, and rubber band guns, to name just a few. These devices were a regular part of any neighborhood kids' arsenal. For example, the slingshot was the go-to weapon for exacting retribution for any slight. There was nothing like a small pebble targeted to the back of some kids' heads to settle a score. The rubber band gun was a gentler approach: a piece of wood shaped like a pistol with a nail trigger, allowing the rubber band to fly and sting someone. Spitballs, most often used at school, could be quickly assembled by chewing a piece of paper and shaping it into a miniature cannonball. Hurriedly constructed, no one was ever defenseless.

My favorite weapon was the "pea shooter." They were ubiquitous in all the stores just before Halloween. Larger than a conventional drinking straw, "the shooter" required a good set of lungs and a mouthful of dried peas. The shotgun spray of hard peas landing on an unsuspecting victim felt like multiple bee stings. Knowing when to inhale and exhale was essential. Any deviation from the breathing sequence caused an unexpected vegetarian meal.

Any game of marbles was another favorite. In front of the Ravlin house, between the sidewalk and the roadside curb, there was a long stretch of packed dirt. It provided a natural marble playground. Everyone had a leather or cloth pouch holding a collection of colored wonders: "clearsies" (see-through one-color glass), boulders about the size of a quarter, and cats' eyes which were clear with a swirl of color inside. Before each game, a quick review of the rules staved off potential arguments. The marbles were tossed gently toward a shallow hole about twelve feet away. Any marbles that didn't go in the hole were then stroked forward across the dirt with the side of an index finger, like a golf putter. An unsuccessful attempt made room for the next player. It was like a game of pool. The most successful marble player was the one who put all the marbles in the hole first.

Most games ended with trades and exchanges of winnings. There were frequent chants of, "I'll give you two clearsies for your boulder with the green streaks in it." We never purchased marbles as there seemed to be an uncanny balance of talent; one kid's loss one day resulted in a winning streak the next. One might be down, but never out.

On rainy days, we busied ourselves with the perpetuation of a private club in the loft of the Ravlin barn. The barn, built in the nineteenth century, had a large attic loft with a wooden staircase to a trap door at the top. Inside were rustic tables, chairs, trunks, and stacks of cardboard boxes. Many of the boxes held files from Ravlin's grandfather, a retired police detective. We spent hours poring through the never-ending collection of 8 x 10 black-and-white crime photos that filled our active imaginations with ideas of murder and espionage. To combat what we were sure was a burgeoning local crime syndicate, we formed our own neighborhood detective agency.

The barn loft also provided a perfect spot for games of strip poker. Calling it "strip poker" was a misnomer. The strip aspect was a fantasy despite the game's intent. It usually depended on whether there were any girls playing. When it was only boys, no one wanted to play.

Palpable was the giddiness of innocence. The anticipation was scintillating, even if nothing memorable ever happened. Each player hoped, "Next time, it might be different."

***

I entered kindergarten at St. Edmond's School, grade school at Mt. Saint Mary's Academy and followed by Cathedral Grammar School. Across the street from the grammar school was the Catholic church. It was a called the Cathedral of the Immaculate Conception and the headquarters of the Catholic Bishop of Vermont. School kids called it "The Cathedral" because no one knew what "immaculate" or "conception" meant.

The Sisters of Mercy ran my school. They encouraged students to sell holiday cards, gift wrapping paper, magazine subscriptions, and candy bars to help raise money for needy Catholic causes. This extracurricular adventure piqued my entrepreneurial spirit. The money raised was to help "Save Pagan Babies," or unbaptized children in Africa. The concept was simple: proceeds from door-to-door sales "won souls" for God and saved the babies from eternal damnation. I worried about the "pagan babies" because their lot in life seemed unfair. They hadn't selected where to be born; God did, so why did they have to be "saved" or damned for life because He couldn't find them? Why would God put these kids in such terrible circumstances?

As a novice salesman, I figured out that "the early bird gets the worm." I skipped door-to-door sales and instead sold piles of Peter Paul Almond Joy candy bars at nearby college dorms and sororities. I politely plied anyone with a free candy bar if they would make an intercom announcement that candy bars were on sale in the lobby. With several cases in hand, I quickly sold everything and went home for more. I never disclosed to the nuns at school how I could possibly sell so much candy. There was no competition. Almost every time, I won the top prize. The reward for increasing the sales for the Hershey Company was a never-ending supply of rosaries and religious books. Eventually, I accumulated enough to surely ascend directly into heaven.

Actually, at a young age, I started talking and never stopped. Relentlessly good at sales, my greatest gift was marketing my own life. I learned that "luck" doesn't work if it isn't used well, and cleverness goes unused if there is no luck. The trick was to grasp the concept; there's luck all around if you're smart enough to recognize it's there. I think I discovered what I might do in life when I noticed what I did well.

As a child, I was never silly. At the age of twelve, I became a paperboy with two paper routes: one in the morning, the *Burlington Free Press*, and one in the evening, the *Burlington Daily News*. Both routes were within walking distance of my home, but in different directions. Delivering papers was when I learned a valuable lesson in business. Each week, I went door to door to collect from my subscribers. Weekly, I had to pay the publishers for the newspapers they gave me. However, not all subscribers paid on time, or they simply weren't home. This left me with no compensation. Occasionally, I had to borrow money from my parents to pay my weekly newspaper debt. Soon, I devised a plan to get subscribers to pay by the month or at least a week in advance. It worked, and I learned a valuable lesson: "You never know unless you ask." Now, I had some money in my pocket.

In addition to modest paper route earnings, my parents gave me three dollars a month for a haircut. Inherently, they knew I would not spend my paper route money on such frivolity. They were right. When it was time for a haircut, I made a beeline to the Shamrock Barber Shop, a short block from school. The shop had *Playboy* magazines. It was a wonderful addition to their library of *Popular Mechanics*, *Saturday Evening Post*, and *Field and Stream*. As a pubescent teen, I thought being able to look at a *Playboy* magazine discreetly tucked inside a Life magazine was too good to be true. I only had to calculate the monthly arrival date for each new issue.

Back at school, the nuns were totally unamused with my antics. In order to wear off some of the excess energy, they encouraged me to perform in the school's theatre program. I was a natural. My first role was the character "Dopey" in *Snow White and the Seven Dwarfs*. All the singing and performing was a perfect fit. When not on the stage, I was at the University of Vermont's Fleming Museum, staring at their ethnographic exhibits of various curiosities from around the world: Egyptian artifacts, mummies, and battle armaments. The cultural displays were arranged theatrically in a darkened room. It seemed like theatre from a different age. I dreamed of being an archaeologist someday so that I could wear khaki clothes and helmets.

At the untethered age of twelve, I joined my neighborhood pals to test our skills at ski jumping. Until then, the most daring thing we'd ever done skiing downhill was fly over a small snow bump, hardly a feat of bravado. A dirt road leading to the University of Vermont's baseball stadium ended abruptly at a steep hill used by the university's ski teams for slalom practice. Adjacent was a twelve-meter ski jump. Absent the UVM ski team, we used the facilities without permission day and night. In the evenings, we merely jerry-rigged the electric wires to flood the ski jump with the university's flood lights.

In the spring and fall, I hunted in the woods behind my East Avenue home. Strolling down the street past my neighbors with my father's twenty-gauge shotgun under my arm, I went hunting for partridge in the nearby woods. I enjoyed the time alone and the inevitable cheers when returning home for dinner with several birds dangling from my belt. My mother knew how to easily remove the breast of the partridge and prepare a delicious meal. The trick was not to break teeth on any pellets that might have been missed in the cleaning process.

One summer, when I was five and at our family's camp, I became friends with Steve McClellan, who was seven. He lived about fifteen minutes away. We called each other "Stevie and Mikie," but no one else ever called us by those names. We were inseparable pals, even after Labor Day when I relocated to my home in Burlington, and rarely saw each other until the next summer. We said our annual goodbyes and our friendship lasted forever.

On especially hot days, we swam in various pools on the mountainside, Stevensville Brook. We pretentiously named one of our favorite swimming holes, "The Marcus Pool," after Shakespeare's "Marcus Aurelius." It was a natural swimming spot, deep and shaped like a bowl with a small waterfall and surrounding rock formations for cannonballing. Our other favorite was Allen's pool, a larger body of water created by means of a sluice gate on a cement dam built long before we were born. Utilizing masks, snorkels, and flippers, we practiced being like a trout and playfully fell off rock outcrops into the water while clutching our chests like wounded cowboys from TV westerns. It was all accomplished with a heady theatrical flourish.

All our swimming holes were fed by a swift mountain stream. The water was never warm. It was characteristically "blue lip" cold. Wading in the water was ridiculous; only jumping in quickly ended the torture. We devised a mandatory "Blue Lip Test." Each was sworn to remind the other when lips turned blue. The individual identified had to lay on a sun-drenched heated rock until natural skin color returned.

Stevie's German Shepard, "Chief," entertained us, or maybe it was the other way around. The dog happily played endless games of "Hide and Seek." We would throw a stick for the dog and then run and hide. The dog, of course, would easily fetch the stick and quickly find us each time. We sometimes thought we had successfully evaded the dog, only to turn and find Chief behind us panting with his tongue hanging out. Chief always had a smile on his face, or at least, I thought it looked like one.

I loved trout fishing by myself. This activity was attractive because I could be alone with my thoughts. No one ever went fishing with me. Neither my pal Stevie nor my father ever accompanied me. This was my domain. My mother loved speckled brook trout. My brimming creel of trout always brought a beaming smile to my mother's face, along with laudatory exclamations. I did this to please my mother. I never ate the fish.

***

As I grew older, smoking and drinking were temptations because they were forbidden. Any birth certificate served as an I.D. to purchase beer. With a birth year of 1947, only the top part of the birth year, "7," had to be erased, so it appeared to be a "1." The results were good enough to purchase the beer needed for most weekend parties. Small struggling neighborhood "Mom and Pop" stores never seemed overly concerned about a fifteen-year-old suggesting he was twenty-one. Realistically, I didn't care that much about drinking, but my other friends did. I'd share one or two beers while some other school pals would polish off a six-pack.

Burlington's North Beach on Lake Champlain was a popular spot for underage beer parties. Police rarely raided the beach area. It was too open and easy for anyone to run away. However, one summer night the police unexpectedly swept North Beach to catch anyone drinking under age twenty-one. The crowd scattered as the police approached. Luckily, I evaded the police by running parallel to the water down the beach. When I was safely out of sight, I simply walked home, elated I had escaped certain doom.

As I strolled home through a grassy field covered with cool evening dew, I noticed a police squad car parked outside my house. Its blue bubble light was flashing. This was not a good sign. Maybe something bad had happened. I hoped my parents were all right. It never occurred to me the police were looking for me. Approaching the door of my house, I was confronted by puzzled parents and two police officers. Unbeknownst to me, one of my captured friends from North Beach had ratted me out in exchange for leniency. The officers queried as to my whereabouts, but the clincher question was, "If you weren't at North Beach, how'd your feet get so wet?" It was a good question, but I had a good answer. Quick on my feet, I calmly described my usual shortcut home across the Mary Fletcher Hospital dew-soaked field. It was an irrefutable response. The police left. My skeptical but relieved parents never talked about the evening again, and I did my best not to remind them.

My interest in music and the arts flourished during my high school years. I enjoyed singing and performing weekend gigs with three high school friends during the popularity of folk groups like the Kingston Trio. We humorously called ourselves "The Lakeshore Four Coach and Buggy Whip Wandering Minstrels" or, more memorably, "The Lakeshore Four." Our group was led by Don "Bud" Villemaire on guitar, Harland Sanders on bass, Mike St. Louis on guitar/banjo and me. My role was to sing harmony and play selected accompanying musical devices such as a kazoo or tambourine. The Lakeshore Four regularly performed at fraternities and sororities, ski resorts, as well as the "The Green Door" in Winooski, Vermont. One of my favorite solo performances was the classic Limelighters rendition of "Have Some Madeira, My Dear." It was a humorous song involving a lecherous old man plying a young girl with noxious sweet wine. It was theatre at its best; my voice wasn't. The compensation was dismal and the psychic rewards were incalculable.

For a few summers, I was a scout leader at the Eden Boy Scout Reservation in East Eden, Vermont. I had been inducted into the prestigious Order of the Arrow and was selected to attend a school at the Mendon Scout Reservation in New Jersey to learn how to teach Scout leadership. Following graduation, I managed a one-week leadership training program for all aspiring junior scout leaders in Vermont. I was sixteen years old and the only Vermonter qualified as a trainer.

But my crowning Boy Scout glory was a stint as a substitute archery instructor. The designated teacher fell ill, and I was asked to step in. My knowledge of archery was sketchy at best, gathered primarily from movies and childhood games of cowboys and Indians. With a cursory review of the archery instruction manual, I felt I could, at least, teach the basics. However, I was unprepared for the first class of young scouts who challenged me to show them "how it's done." It was a provocation I hadn't expected. "Show us the way *you* hit the target, Michael," the scouts exclaimed. I wondered what made them think I couldn't. Maybe they knew I wasn't an expert.

I gulped more than once. This was going to be an unintended defining moment. Word would quickly spread if I missed the target. Ever the confident performer, I drew back my bow, said "Hail Mary," and let the arrow fly. It went straight into the bullseye. There was an audible gasp from the scouts and also from me. I was flabbergasted but tried to carefully mask the bulk of my surprise. "Nothing like a straight arrow," I suggested triumphantly. Word spread fast, and I became a legend. From that day forth, no other scout ever asked me to demonstrate my archery prowess again. It was a total mystery to me how I did it. Determined to go out on top, I never picked up a bow and arrow again.

~ 3 ~

YOUNG, FOOLISH, AND FORGIVEN

After high school, I packed my belongings to go to college.

My parents drove me to Johnson State College (now Vermont State University), about an hour away. I settled into my new dorm room with a roommate who was my old neighborhood friend, Tony Lizotte, from East Avenue. We felt fortunate to be able to bunk together. The dorm room, a humble space with overhead bunks, a desk underneath, and a closet for clothes, was spare, bland, and compact. Eventually, we agreed to decorate the dorm room with a few beer signs and *Playboy* centerfolds in tribute to my halcyon memories from the Shamrock Barber Shop.

One momentous September day, my parents appeared at my dorm room unannounced. Fortunately, I was not there to witness my mother's amazement and disappointment with my degenerative room decor. I learned from Tony that my father was still staring at the centerfolds on the wall when my mother nudged him in the ribs with the admonition to stop looking and prepare a disapproving note for me before they left.

Dear Michael,

We were surprised not to find you here when we came for a visit to take you out for dinner. Instead, it was we who were surprised!

Needless to say, we were startled to see your dorm room festooned with beer cartons and naked women. This was a shock. It was not the way we raised you and we had higher expectations. Remember such acts are not only a reflection on you, but also on your family.

With love,

Dad and Mom

My first college semester was a disaster. The failure was all my own doing. I had unwittingly engineered my own demise in four different ways: First, I flunked as many classes as I passed. Mathematics and chemistry were albatrosses. Second, my roommate Tony and I got caught one Saturday night sharing a sixteen-ounce can of beer while playing a game of cribbage in our room. We only had one beer. It was all we could afford. However, this was a major infraction. Third, Tony and I created a giant icicle outside our dorm room window. The long icicle was gleefully sculpted by pouring pitcher after pitcher of different shades of colored water each night from our window down the side of the building. It froze instantly. The result was a 28-foot-long ice rainbow from their third-floor window to the ground. It never occurred to us it would be easy to determine who was responsible. Perhaps this fact alone was worthy of dismissal. Finally, the crowning "coup de grâce" was my role in falsifying a nomination for President of the College Ski Club. The first meeting was held to identify nominations for president. No one was nominated. Nobody wanted the job. Wanting to be funny, I raised my hand and nominated an "imaginary candidate" to lighten the mood. Pressed for details, I quickly made up an imaginary candidate. Unfortunately, everyone believed me and elected the candidate as their club President. I simply didn't have the guts to tell them it was a joke. They were all so satisfied.

My college suspension letter arrived during the Christmas holiday break. It suggested, for a number of reasons, not altogether limited to those already recounted, that I was found to be an unsuitable student and would not be invited back for the second semester.

This wasn't a shock to me as much as it was to my parents. They had taken out college loans, so they were most unhappy, embarrassed, and disappointed. Hurriedly, plans were made for me to make up flunked college courses with evening classes at the nearby University of Vermont. The strategy was to demonstrate mature remorse so the College might take me back.

***

While I was at Johnson State, I dated fellow freshman, Barbara Benzie. She was a recent transplant from Texas to Vermont. Her father had been transferred to the IBM plant in Essex Jct., Vermont. We saw each other regularly during the fall term and after my college dismissal, on weekends, despite the distance. As the relationship grew, living with my parents cramped the regularity of our dating. Our time together was always tempered by the availability of a fifty-mile roundtrip in our family car.

One cool date night, Barbara and I decided we wanted some private time. We drove to a dark corner of an empty high school parking lot, away from prying eyes. The heated kissing and fumbling veered toward an as yet unexplored place. We had most of our clothes off, the car windows were steamed opaque, and the night was young.

A few months later, Barbara announced she was pregnant. I was bowled over. She hadn't mentioned anything about feeling funny or being suspicious about physical changes.

"What are we going to do?" she asked earnestly. We were scared. Eventually, we talked to our parents because we had only three choices: get an abortion, one or both of us raise the child on our own, or quickly get married. The married option seemed the wisest choice under the circumstances.

"Are you sure about this?" Barbara wondered.

I knew this was a time to reassure her and move forward with our commitment. "I am sure," I said. "I wouldn't want to embark on this journey with anyone but you."

We sent invitations to family members and friends for a hurried June 11, 1966, wedding ceremony at a church near Barbara's parents' home in Essex Junction. My best friends, schoolmates, and cousins were chosen to be either altar boys, the best man, or ushers, while Barbara picked family members and friends for her entourage. The wedding reception was held in the backyard of Barbara's home. It was a bewildering capstone to the day. Barbara was about three and a half months pregnant.

After a weekend honeymoon at Lake George, Vermont, we temporarily moved into a spare room in my parent's home in Burlington. The plan was for us to live there until other arrangements could be made. I quickly found a job working at Rocheleau Decorating Company in Winooski and became the manager of the company's warehouse and inventory, loading and unloading trucks with a forklift for different scheduled jobs. I was now a husband and soon-to-be father. I was scared and unsure if I was ready.

On November 21, 1966, Sean Michael Luck was born at the Bishop DeGoesbriand Hospital. Unlike contemporary men, expectant fathers remained in the waiting room until someone announced the birth. Every new father was rushed down the hallway to hug the mother, hold the baby, and quickly depart so everyone could rest. It was a whirlwind moment of daunting excitement. By then, nineteen, neither of us knew what we were doing. Perhaps, at any age, no one does.

Sean, a handsome child, appeared without complications with all fingers and toes. I was proud, if not overwhelmed. The enormity of what had occurred hit me like a lightning bolt. I thought about the ways my son would grow and imagined how best to be a father. Now, I had a new lifetime assignment, neither debatable nor negotiable. It was the day I became a man and as close to the best father I could be. I felt like I was still in foreign territory. Restlessly contemplating my son's birth, the trajectory of our new family was set. No matter how I viewed my life as a father, the answer was clear: it was the best thing that would ever happen to me. The big question was, "What kind of father would I become?" There was a lot of growing up to do.

The Vietnam War compelled my enlistment in the Vermont Army National Guard. The Guard provided me with a way to participate in military service while married with a child and extra income. I made the most of my six-year commitment to the Guard by applying for Officer's Candidate School. The school was completed on assigned weekends in lieu of regular Guard duty. A year later, I was commissioned as a second lieutenant and remained in the National Guard and Army Reserves for twelve years, with appointments in Vermont, Illinois, and Massachusetts.

***

Fortunately, both of our parents provided enormous financial and emotional support to us. However, living with parents was not an optimal long-term solution. Barbara's parents had constructed a new home in the Town of Underhill. Evelyn Benzie was a wonderful grandmother, frequently helping with Sean's care and inviting us to dinner. During this time, I spoke with Barbara's father.

"Our family is growing, and we definitely need a home of our own. What should we do?"

"I've heard good things about Flanders homes," he said.

The Flanders Lumber Company, in 1967, advertised a special low-cost ranch house. The company promised to erect a three-bedroom ranch over a crawl space with a carport for $9,999. The buyer was responsible for the building lot, water, and sewer. It seemed like a bargain for our first home.

With the Flanders Lumber Company contract, I purchased five hillside acres of land from Kent Rawson, a farmer, near the Benzie's Underhill home. My parents helped finance the construction of the Flanders home by extending a credit line on their existing Burlington residence on East Avenue so we had a manageable monthly payment plan. In the spring of 1967, the home was completed, and we happily moved in with baby Sean. Barbara's parents were still nearby and continued to be most attentive.

Within a month, I wrote an official letter to Johnson State College, respectfully asking to be readmitted, describing my dramatically altered life circumstances since my dismissal. The college quickly responded and suggested I would be welcomed back. In the evenings, Barbara worked as an operator at the Burlington Telephone Company, while I held several part-time jobs around classes during the day. I learned a lot working for a Fire Damage Restoration Company, cleaning smoke film from ceilings, walls, and floors, painting the interior and exterior of houses and commercial properties, and installing antennas on roofs of homes and buildings for a TV and appliance center near the college. I was paid a high fee for my willingness to scramble up steep slate roofs and attach antennas to brick chimneys. My best part-time job was at IBM, where Barbara's parents were employed. It was much safer. I cleaned computer disks before they were manufactured into chips. The combination of day and evening shifts worked well for Sean's care. Nearby, Barbara's parents always volunteered to babysit their first grandson when needed.

Tackling college with a flourish, I took heavy course loads each semester to finish as soon as possible. I completed all my studies in 1970 with all A's (a remarkable academic turnaround from my initial effort.) I earned a bachelor's degree in three years with high honors and became a Woodrow Wilson Fellow nominee.

While finishing college, my old high school friend, Jerry Durick, gave me some advice.

"Why don't you apply to graduate school at Southern Illinois University (SIU) at Carbondale, Illinois? As you know, I'm working on my master's degree in English, and it's a great school."

As with any major life decision, I solicited advice from Barbara, who was quite supportive. "My father always said there's no investment like education."

With that, I decided there was nothing to lose. I submitted an application to SIU and Cornell University. While waiting, I was offered a high school teaching job at nearby Mount Mansfield Union

High School, followed by letters of acceptance to graduate school from Cornell University and SIU for study in Anthropology (my time in the Fleming Museum paid off.) This was a bit of a surprise as neither of us thought my applications had much chance. Cornell attendance would have been closer to Vermont, but the financial package from SIU made the choice easy. The university offered a teaching assistantship with free graduate tuition and a monthly stipend for living expenses like rent and groceries. We decided to accept. Baby Sean was four years old, and Barbara was pregnant with another baby, which was due in late November.

We arrived in Carbondale and settled into our assigned married graduate student housing. Our second-floor two-bedroom apartment was pleasant, with a small terrace and plenty of other students with children. It was almost like a private club with all members in similar circumstances. The transition from a rural life in Vermont, with family nearby, to living in an apartment surrounded by hundreds of strangers was an adjustment. We were really on our own for the first time.

On December 4, 1970, Barbara delivered a beautiful baby daughter with large expressive eyes, and we named her Holly Marie Luck. She was supposed to be named "Kelly," but Barbara's due date in late November slipped into early December, prompting consideration of a new name. If son Sean's birth helped us quickly mature, Holly's arrival sealed the deal. I was thrilled with my growing family, and four-year-old Sean found his new baby sister's lack of hair a source of amazement and entertainment.

Barbara found part-time work selling Sarah Coventry jewelry through home shows with recruited gracious hosts. The work was not only rewarding but also provided a social outlet. Our large graduate student apartment complex supplied an optimal audience for fun evenings of trying on and buying inexpensive jewelry. Her work was flexible, usually involving evenings when I was home.

My service in the Army National Guard continued in both East St. Louis and West Frankfort, Illinois coupled with my duties as a teaching assistant at the university. Soon, my role in the National Guard became awkward. There were frequent Vietnam War protests in Carbondale adjacent to the SIU campus and my unit was called more than once to quell public disturbances and halt public property damage.

Guardsmen were expected to discourage and disperse students with a show of overwhelming military resolve and strength. Naturally, the students demonstrated fortitude with taunts and occasional hurled items, but most fled when armed formations moved closer. Others stayed until the last minute until they realized the guardsmen would not back down. I hated this part of my job, but it was my responsibility. Sometimes, some of my fellow students and friends would recognize me and yell, "Hey, Luck, what the hell are you doing? We thought you were our friend?"

My reply was always, "I'm just doing my job. Please leave so you don't get hurt."

***

Within two years, I completed my master's degree in Anthropology with a thesis on "The Preliminary Foundation of Puluwatan Navigational Cognition," which provided insight into the cognitive learning process used by South Sea Islanders to acquire unique heuristic sailing tactics.

Unfortunately, it was determined that no one in the Anthropology Department was capable of overseeing my doctoral study and dissertation in my chosen field of cognitive/educational theory. A decision was made to create a hybrid degree combining Anthropology and Education with a newly designated dissertation chair. I was quickly admitted into the doctoral program in the Department of Higher Education.

As I began my doctoral studies, I met the president of the university, David R. Derge, at a campus social occasion. "It's been quite an adventure for us since leaving Vermont," I told him. He listened intently and seemed to understand my plight as a young father and husband making his way through the world of academia.

About a month later, I received a call. "The President would like to see you about an important matter."

When I arrived at his office, the university president warmly welcomed me. "I really enjoyed our previous conversation, and I have a proposal for you if you'd indulge me."

"Certainly," I replied. "I'm all ears."

"I'm working on a plan to broaden my public image and project greater accessibility. To that end, would you consider continuing your doctoral studies and accepting a position with my office? Your title would be Special Assistant to the President and Vice President for External Affairs, with a compensation of $13,500 a year. Of course, you would be free to continue your coursework and keep all existing graduate tuition support."

"Yes, I'd be honored," I responded rather quickly. I regretted my haste because Barbara and I always agreed to discuss important decisions together to make sure we were in total agreement.

Fortunately, she was as supportive as I'd hoped. She even suggested we celebrate our good fortune by moving out of graduate student housing and buying a house. It would be a smart move for our growing family, so we quickly found a ranch house near campus. Now, Sean and Holly had a backyard playground and new neighborhood friends.

At the university, I ramped up external relations for the president by creating a weekly live television show featuring him with special guests at SIU's television and radio studios. A local furniture store donated the set for the show while I produced and directed the entire affair. It was just like theatre, which I loved. I was twenty-five years old.

Coupled with the television show, I boosted the university's planned "Silver Anniversary International Air Show" in coordination with the university's Aviation and Flight School by inviting Neil Armstrong and Bill Lear (Lear Jets) as special guests. They represented the past, present, and future of aviation.

Soon, I also started a weekly column in the student newspaper called "Answering Letters by David R. Derge." The newspaper column, combined with scheduled outings to fraternities and sororities on campus and his own TV show, happily built an external presence for the president. With momentum, I recommended a "Second Chance Program" for students to expunge poor academic performance during a semester in exchange for a fresh start. From my time at Johnson State College, I was sympathetic to students who make mistakes. A number of students applied for the opportunity to cancel a semester of bad grades because of a death in the family, a relationship breakup, or illness. The concept was simple: "Everybody deserves a second chance."

Near the completion of my doctorate, I was offered a job at Ottumwa Heights Community College in Iowa. It was located in a fairly remote area of Iowa. I accepted the interview even though I was skeptical. Ottumwa Heights College President Jerry Solloway asked if one of my direct supervisors would write a letter of recommendation. The Vice President of Development and Services, T. Richard Mager, humorously penned an "Academy Award-winning" tongue-in-cheek letter.

30 March 1973
Dear President Solloway,
I am certainly surprised Michael Luck would have the gall to ask me to recommend him for any position. However, since he has seen fit to do so, I feel I must write with honesty and candor about his shortcomings and miserable failures during his tenure on my staff."

The letter went on for pages describing missteps and mistakes that were actually clever decisions and tactics.

I received a job offer but declined. Ottumwa, Iowa, was not in the direction I wanted to go, and I was unsure where such a position might lead. I had bigger ambitions while Barbara pined for a location back in New England. She missed her parents.

I adjusted my plans for my dissertation and conducted a nationwide study of development programs in public community colleges. It was the first such comprehensive U.S. survey ever undertaken. My study was entitled "Community College Development: Alternative Fundraising Strategies." Eventually, the doctoral dissertation became a book and won national recognition, and I completed my PhD.

~ 4 ~

A NOMADIC LIFE

Completing my doctoral studies at SIU Carbondale coincided with the imminent departure of the university's president.

The unraveling of the university's administration moved my office to a more discreet location off campus. This was my first taste of high-stakes university politics. When presidents depart, new leaders prefer their own senior executives. The tenure average for university presidents had been about five years. This suggests the advent of a nomadic life if I were to stay in higher education administration.

Thankfully, in 1974, the Massachusetts Institute of Technology (MIT) announced it was seeking an assistant development officer. My work as a special assistant to the SIU president involved many fundraising and development aspects, so I applied for the position. Luckily, MIT called. An official announced the search for candidates had ended, but the committee determined my résumé warranted last-minute attention. Luck would have it that I interviewed and received a job offer. I was astounded. The MIT position cemented my commitment to philanthropic management for nonprofit institutions. The position at MIT catapulted my professional life.

Barbara was ecstatic. "We can move back to New England," she said gleefully. "It's where we belong."

We purchased a lovely home in Tewksbury, Massachusetts, located in a good school district. We moved East in the late summer of 1974. All was in place for a new beginning.

The job at MIT was ideal. Settled happily, the biggest surprise came six months later when the Director of the Office of Development accepted a position at the Yale New Haven Medical Center. MIT announced a search for a new Director, and I was asked if I would consider serving as the "acting" Director until a suitable candidate was selected. I said, "Absolutely."

Several months later, MIT's Executive Director for Institutional Advancement asked me to lunch. "The search for a new Director of the Development Office has been completed," he said as coffee was served.

"So, who is it?"

The Executive Director leaned forward and said, "Michael, a decision has been made and agreed upon by the MIT President, the Chairman of the Corporation, and the Institute's Trustees that you should be appointed as the new Director if you'll accept."

I spewed my coffee. It was the last thing I expected to hear. I had been at MIT for less than a year. In a surprised swirl of emotions, I said, "Yes, totally, yes," and quickly apologized for the mess. Now, my real leadership skills would be tested. A new $225 million "MIT Leadership Campaign" had just been launched.

While at MIT, I interacted with many professors and administrators, including "Doc" Edgerton (the "father" of stop-action photography), Jay Forrester (a father of the modern computer as well as "System Dynamics"), and Professor Samuel Goldblith, the former Chair of the Food and Nutrition Department, who was helping to lead the campaign. A survivor of the infamous Bataan Death March in Japan, he was universally recognized as one of the "founding fathers" of the freeze-dried method for storing food. I had the privilege of co-authoring an article with him I had written in *The International Journal of Food Technology*. Published in 1977, the article was entitled "Man's Food Supply in Ancient Times: Some Aspects of Preservation Indicated by Archaeological Remains."

***

While my role at MIT continued to be rewarding, my ten-year marriage was unraveling. Among our other issues, Barbara was not excited about my new position when she realized that it would likely mean more relocations. Her hope was to make a permanent home in Vermont near her parents. After ten years of marriage and two and a half years in Massachusetts, we decided to separate and take some time to try and work out our differences.

So, in January of 1976, I rented a room in a classic old Cambridge home near Harvard, owned by an elderly woman who provided accommodations for several graduate students. Until that moment, I had never spent much time wondering what I wanted for myself. I felt I had met an attractive, smart woman, developed a relationship, and begun a solid life together. Then, I embarked on a career that absorbed whatever talents I had, and I made a success of it. I'd been able to provide for my family, but if there had ever been a fork in the road, I hadn't noticed it. Maybe that was part of the problem. All I'd ever done was put one foot in front of the other and kept walking. I felt that if I stopped moving for even a moment, someone might knock me over.

My professional life had become frightening and perilous. My dedication to staying employed increasingly took precedence over spending quality time with my family. I had been raised at a time when the emphasis was on providing for the family. There was less focus on learning how to nurture relationships and develop strong bonds with our children. The expectation was that if you made a good living, the rest would fall into place. Ours was also the classic tale of two young people who simply grew apart. In our teens, life was simple, and our needs easily met. As we matured, I spent most of my time around the mannered intellectuals discussing philosophical and worldly events. Barbara's sensibilities remained a bit more provincial in nature, and she was uninterested in the professional world that I found so fulfilling. She sought less disruption; she wanted a simpler life.

It was especially heartbreaking since Sean (ten) and Holly (six) were naturally confused, unsure about the future and what separation meant for them and their parents. It was an extremely sad, difficult time for all of us. No one was emotionally prepared to deal with feelings of hurt and disappointment. Explaining to my children, as best I could, why I would not be coming home each night was crushing. I tried to convince them I would still see them, but we all knew things might never be the same.

Barbara called one day, suggesting the children wanted to see me a day earlier than planned and could I come immediately after work? Naturally, I agreed. Soon there was a knock at the front door. Barbara answered it and yelled, "Michael, it's for you."

That's when the local Tewksbury sheriff served me with divorce papers just as Barbara's father appeared at the top of the stairs, where he had been hiding out of sight since my arrival. I was stunned, bewildered, and in shock. I simply never saw this coming. Separation was one thing, but divorce had not been seriously discussed. This was a giant, uncontemplated next step. Confused, I hugged my children and quickly concluded my visit without revealing what had happened. I told them I'd see them the next day as planned.

Barbara's attorney, as was customary, requested both monthly alimony and child support for our children, as well as sole ownership of the Tewksbury house. I did not argue or negotiate. I instructed my attorney to accept whatever seemed reasonable and fair. The safety and security of my children was most important.

Barbara's final request was another shock, full custody of the children. I understood why Barbara's father pushed to initiate divorce proceedings. With full custody she would be free to sell the Tewksbury house, start a new life with Sean and Holly near her father and mother in Vermont. Full custody meant there would be no court fights over moving out of state with Sean and Holly.

After continued legal wrangling, an agreement was reached allowing Barbara to move out of state, and I would be able to see my children anytime and anywhere outside of school with respectful notice.

The divorce, based on irreconcilable differences, was painful. Heartbroken and fearing the damage to my children became a crippling obsession. I cried often not totally for Barbara, the children, or me but for the death of a marriage, which was an inconsolable loss. I sensed when I left my children that I would be forever separated, and I was.

***

Months later, I was working hard at MIT and adjusting to my single life; I received a telephone call from Dr. Donald Tolle, the chair of my doctoral dissertation committee. We quickly updated each other about personal and professional news and the sadness of my divorce. I was delighted to hear a positive voice from the past. We discussed the idea of reworking my dissertation into a book as co-authors. I agreed and made contact with R & R Newkirk, a national charitable gift consulting company that regularly published boutique books for two-year colleges. R & R Newkirk embraced the idea of publishing the book and suggested it would be widely available and publicized nationally.

It was exciting that *Community College Development: Alternative Fundraising-Strategies* was published and released in early 1978. The book sold well and won national recognition from the National Society of Fundraising Executives (NSFRE) and was placed in their "National Heritage Collection." It became an esteemed book in the field of philanthropy.

***

While at MIT from 1974 to 1978, I met Dean Irwin Sizer, an adviser for the institute's fundraising campaign, and his Executive Assistant, Barbara Wilson. Over time, Barbara Wilson and I would have lunch and sometimes dinner together. We enjoyed each other's company. In 1978, I was asked to consider a position as

President of the Rutgers University Foundation in New Brunswick, New Jersey. An old friend and colleague suggested I take a look at it. It would be a big step up, and I would have nothing to lose by throwing my hat into the ring. Although content at MIT, the new position reported to the President of Rutgers University as well as a separate Foundation Board. This, for me, would be a big change and an introduction to a major leadership role.

But what about my budding relationship with Barbara Wilson? I found myself at a crossroads, personally and professionally. The new job was a slam dunk, but a romantic commitment took more thought. Did I want to dip my toes into the unpredictable waters of marriage once again? Was Barbara willing to leave MIT and move with me to New Jersey? Were either of us prepared to remarry after failed relationships? Barbara was very attractive, intelligent, and adventuresome. She was socially experienced, and that would help facilitate my career aspirations as well as her own career. She was ambitious to finish her formal education. We were in love.

Barbara was accustomed to frequent moves and the rewards of getting to know new places. After completing her Associate of Arts degree in 1967 at Stephens College, Columbia, Missouri, she moved to Europe and continued her studies. She visited friends of the family in Munich, Germany, who recommended she study German at the Goethe Institute, located in Schloss Gracht, Euskirchen, just outside of Bonn/Bad Godesburg, the sitting capital of Germany, during initial post-WWII years, later returned to Berlin. After four months of study, she moved to Frankfurt am Main and continued her academic studies in Philology at the Johann Wolfgang Goethe University. After a few years, Barbara moved to Valencia, Spain, where she continued her studies while working for a real estate development company.

"Barbara, I was offered the Rutgers job today!"

"Michael, that's great news! I'm so excited for you. I know it's what you wanted."

"That's true," I said, "but of course it means relocating to New Jersey. Will you come with me? I can't imagine doing this with anyone else."

"Of course I will," she said.

"There's just one little hitch, so to speak."

"What's that?"

"With all of the social requirements, it would be better all the way around if we were actually married. What do you say?"

"Michael, are you trying to propose?"

"Sorry, Barbara, I just think of us as a couple already, but you are quite right. Miss Barbara Wilson, would you do me the honor of becoming my wife?"

"Yes, Mr. Luck, I would like that very much!"

We laughed and hugged as we talked of the changes our lives would soon take. Because of the tight timeline I was on, we decided upon a civil ceremony, which took place May 31, 1978, during our lunch hour. Barbara and I walked to the nearby Cambridge Town Hall, where we were married by a Justice of the Peace. It was a two-minute ceremony that withstood the test of time! However, we weren't going to eschew tradition completely. We decided to share our excitement with our families. Several weeks later, on Martha's Vineyard, we were married again! Our parents, Bill and Mary Luck and Carroll and Mary Wilson, were in attendance, as were Barbara's niece, Colby, and, most importantly, Sean and Holly. Wilson family friends, pastors Drs. David and Elizabeth Dodson Gray, officiated our wedding ceremony on June 24. It was a warm and happy moment as Barbara and I embarked on this new journey together.

***

Once established in my new position at Rutgers University, it was clear my schedule would not afford enough time to continue my twelve-year commission in the Army National Guard. As an Army officer, my promotions increased the amount of time required for service. It became difficult to balance required work responsibilities with the increasing demands of military leadership. I was satisfied with my experience in the service and enjoyed fellow guardsmen and the jointly shared experiences of rescue and recovery operations during Mississippi River floods, Vietnam War protests, Midwest tornadoes, and even the Boston blizzard of 1978. I had done my duty and served double the mandatory six-year term.

When it came time to find a new home, we settled on a 200-year-old farmhouse, located in Neshanic Station, New Jersey. We were fascinated by our historic home, its provenance and the local history of the surrounding area. I knew it was the one when we took the tour, and I saw Barbara's reaction.

"Michael, it's beautiful. Look at the amazing fruit trees, a place for a swing, an outdoor fireplace, even a rhubarb patch!"

While I toiled away at Rutgers, Barbara successfully completed her undergraduate degree at nearby Thomas Edison College in Trenton, NJ. Her bachelor's degree had been a long process.

During those years, most universities required students to complete at least two years of study in residence at their institutions before awarding an academic degree. Thomas Edison offered Barbara an opportunity to consolidate all her college credits into a Modern Language bachelor's in arts degree without the two-year residency. She graduated in 1979. She was accepted into the Rutgers University Graduate School and was awarded an M.Ed. degree in Adult Education and Continuing Education with a Certificate in Gerontology in 1980.

During that time, I found myself in the midst of a political firestorm with the Rutgers University Foundation Treasurer. Instead of succumbing to the workplace chaos, I chose to quietly resign and take some time off to regroup. Our lives had been moving at such a fast clip that we hadn't focused on ourselves. So, we sold our historic home, packed up our belongings, and hit the road.

The time between jobs was invaluable. It offered Barbara and me the opportunity to plan a special summer trip to Europe and bring Sean and Holly with us. It would be one of my first trips overseas.

Barbara's knowledge of Europe and linguistic ability would help us navigate our journey.

The European trip was epic. We landed in Valencia, Spain, where Barbara had lived for a few years. After adjusting to the time change, we joined her ex-husband and his family for Valencian paella as one and all roamed the beach by the Mediterranean Sea. Then, we visited the Provence in southern France. We rented a home in a local village, Le Beausset, not far from the Mediterranean, and made frequent trips back and forth to the beach. Sean and Holly were enthralled with all the new experiences.

From Provence, we made our way to Italy for a very special encounter. One highlight for the children (other than playing on the beach or building walls on ancient terraces) was to meet their great aunt, Señora Treves (Benzie), in St. Vincent, Italy. Given a sketchy address and no phone information as a lead, it was a tour de force to find her. Eventually, given Barbara's ingenuity and general ability to pull together leads from Kiosks and passersby, we found Senora Treves' hotel, "The African Play." She had no idea we were seeking her out. After several inquiries, Barbara successfully located the hotel, and our entourage made our way there. We achieved entry into the hotel and navigated down corridors with 30-second hall lights. Finally, we located Señora Treves' door. We knocked. By and by, the heavy door swung open, and an elderly, impeccably groomed, stocky woman stood before us. At first, she was skeptical about who we were, as we probably appeared to be wayward wanderers. That was until Barbara successfully communicated in Spanish/Italian sufficient information as to who we were.

Once she understood that the children by our sides were her great niece and nephew from the United States, a wide smile greeted us, and her eyes opened wide as saucers! She said, "Buon pomeriggio!" She gestured for us to enter immediately and excitedly shared her thrill and amazement at meeting us. We were welcomed in a warm and engaging manner, and we had outstanding food and drink and meetings with family members and friends from the village. Barbara valiantly facilitated conversations and translations back and forth from English, Italian, and Spanish. At Senora Treves' insistence that night, we slept on deliciously fresh linen sheets at The African Play. The moment was magical and unforgettable.

***

After our European trip, I was offered a position as Senior Vice President for Development and Public Affairs at Wayne State University in Detroit, Michigan. The university, the largest public, urban, single-campus university in the U.S. with 33,000 students, also had the largest medical school. We settled in Grosse Pointe Park, and two years later, our beautiful son, Jonathan Wilson Luck, was born on June 7, 1982. Barbara continued her studies in a Doctoral Program in Educational Administration at WSU. As my new responsibilities evolved, entertaining and representing the university at regional events became more frequent, and Barbara became fully immersed in the art of social engagements. It was a happy time. My relationship with the university president was wonderful, and once again, I advanced my professional experience in senior administration at a top research university. Jonathan was an adorable, smart, happy child who had two older siblings with an age gap between twelve and sixteen years.

~ 5 ~

THE UNINVITED APPARITION

In 1985, my career continued to blossom and allowed me to, once again, pack my adoption thoughts away.

After five years at Wayne State University, I accepted a position with the Healtheast Healthcare System in Allentown, Pennsylvania. Healthcare was a slight career shift, but one I enjoyed. Barbara, and I with young son, Jonathan (now, age three) moved into an historic Pennsylvania Dutch home with a classic bank barn. The large rural country location made it ideal to host social occasions, unique and colorful hospital events as well as to wander haplessly through the woods to unimaginably amazing neighborhood peach orchards.

Whenever I changed jobs, I was frequently required to complete numerous life insurance forms as part of my compensation package. This always raised the question of adoption. The forms for insurance requested information about my biological parents. The information would be used to project likely lifespan and health trajectories. Each job change reminded me of that absence in my life. I did not know anything about them, and maybe it would be helpful to at least be familiar with their lineage and health background at some point.

While Barbara was writing her doctoral dissertation, she found a spritely, sixty-year-old woman named Mrs. McFetridge to care for Jonathan, who was four years old and attending Montessori School.

Mrs. McFetridge was the widow of a retired Army general, and every day, she arrived impeccably dressed in her enormous ancient Cadillac.

Over the summer of 1986, Mrs. McFetridge shared pieces of her life with Barbara. One day, she pulled her aside and spoke sotto voce, even though they were the only two in the house. "I just want to share with you that I'm actually a psychic."

Barbara smiled sweetly, indulging her to see where it would go. "Is that a fact? What exactly does that mean?"

"Well, I have the ability to see things in the future. For example, as a young woman, I predicted the sinking of a WWII battleship."

"Oh, my," Barbara said. "Well, you know, speaking of being psychic, when we purchased the home, the previous owners did mention that they thought it was inhabited by a friendly ghost. They noted that garden tools and implements would be moved to different places but never found an accomplice. The ghost was said to be an old Pennsylvania Dutch farmer."

Mrs. McFetridge leaned in. "Honestly, I'm not surprised. If I'm being honest, I've already noted a ghost's movements in the house." Later, Barbara shared the conversation with me; I could tell she was increasingly intrigued, while I remained more than doubtful.

One morning, Mrs. McFetridge arrived a bit tired and uncharacteristically disheveled. Barbara asked, "You don't appear to be well today. Are you OK?"

Mrs. McFetridge explained, "Well, I'm not sure. Yesterday, as I was driving down your driveway on my way home, I met him."

"You met who, exactly?" Barbara asked.

"Why, the ghost, of course. He was seated on a rock on the left side of the driveway. He urgently flagged me down and asked to enter my car. He had something important to tell me. Believe me that is not as unusual as it sounds. They often want to talk when they find someone they can communicate with," Mrs. McFetridge said with satisfaction. "However, this was quite different because I drove home and parked in the driveway. He talked until 4:00 in the morning! Can you imagine?"

Ever the pragmatist, Barbara was picturing her nanny in her oversized Cadillac, speaking to an imaginary spirit.

Mrs. McFetridge implored, "I know this may be difficult to digest, but it's important because I found out what the ghost wanted to tell me. He said that a member of your family will be involved in a serious accident!"

She paused, waiting for a response. Barbara was momentarily speechless while wrapping her head around this new revelation. "Please, go on."

Mrs. McFetridge asked Barbara, "Would you mind if I read some Tarot cards for you?"

Although Barbara had only once had her fortune told at an amusement park, she agreed. "Sure, if you think it will help."

The two sat at our dining table, and Mrs. McFetridge laid the cards on the table. Slowly turning over each card, she asked, "Are you planning a trip?"

"Not really, unless it has to do with driving Jonathan and his classmates on a planned overnight camping trip."

Mrs. McFetridge paused and closed her eyes. "No, that's not it. The cards are saying it's about a man, a woman, and death."

Barbara told her the only other planned trip was the annual drive her in-laws, Bill and Mary Luck, made from their Florida home to the Luck camp in Vermont. They always traveled by car to enjoy the annual change of scenery. My mother, especially, loved the anticipation of the cool mountain air, rural life, and a chance to relish her roots.

It was at that moment that Mrs. McFetridge spoke, "That's it, the cards see a fatal car accident in Georgia. I'm very sorry that I have to deliver this news, but I feel you should know."

"Yes, of course." Barbara was shocked and horrified by the thought.

Mrs. McFetridge seemed relieved to finally relay the ghost's message despite its grim prediction. She asked Barbara, "Is there any way you can convince them not to drive? Is there some other way for them to get to Vermont? This accident must be avoided."

Barbara immediately called me and shared Mrs. McFetridge's prediction. Although my belief in foreseeing unknown events was nearly nonexistent, I agreed we should err on the side of caution. Such a tragedy would be unforgivable. We made a plan to ask my parents if they would allow Barbara to drive them to Vermont. My parents promptly agreed! Their eager response seemed providential, and my appreciation for Mrs. McFetridge grew immensely.

As my parents prepared for Barbara's arrival, they realized their car couldn't hold three adults, a dog, and all the clothes and supplies they needed for their summer. A new plan was quickly devised. Bill would take a train from Florida to Washington, D.C., and then change trains to Philadelphia, where I would pick him up and transport him to our Zionsville home. A bit later, Barbara, Mary, and the dog would arrive by car. Then, we would all travel to Vermont in two cars so Barbara and I could drive back. The plan made sense. Bill secured a train ticket, and the plan unfurled.

While everyone was in transit, I received a telephone call from my father. He had missed his train connection to Philadelphia and didn't know what to do. He had successfully taken the train to Washington, D.C., but was frightened and confused. I suggested he stay by the railroad ticket office, and I would come pick him up. He agreed with relief. I drove as quickly as possible, and fortunately, I found him safe and sound, if not a little rattled. This was my first real sense he was developing a degree of cognitive impairment, an inability to problem-solve and deal with setbacks and complexities. Together, we rode back to Pennsylvania, and after a good dinner, my father slept for more than ten hours. Barbara, my mother, and the dog arrived safely the next day.

***

In what seemed like a trend, Barbara and I were packing to move from Pennsylvania to El Paso, Texas, in the summer of 1992. The President and my friend at Healtheast, David Buchmueller, had resigned to accept a new position at the only public, not-for-profit hospital in El Paso. David invited me for a brief consulting visit and then asked if I would be interested in taking up the torch to assist the city and its residents by raising funds for the hospital. We had already worked together for seven years. After a tour of El Paso, I walked across the bridge to Ciudad Juarez, Mexico, with David to his favorite restaurant, Martino's. Like all good friends, after a few drinks and a delicious meal, it was time to decide whether to take the job. I said I was very interested as it was suggested Barbara would also be employed. However, I thought Barbara should also visit to see if she would be happy there. David agreed. Soon, Barbara arrived in El Paso. She loved it! So, the deal was closed.

Once again, we packed up our household and, along with Jonathan, took up residence in El Paso. Our new home had an enormous swimming pool, where we basked under sunny, if not hot, skies and enjoyed a summer exploring our new city and the Southwest. Barbara soon joined the hospital to work with the International Marketing Program in North Central Mexico, as well as founding, in conjunction with Texas Tech Medical School, a medical residency program.

Given our past Mrs. McFetridge premonition, the following spring, Barbara asked my parents if they were planning their annual trip North to Vermont. She asked, "I'm just wondering if you might enjoy some assistance traveling, like last year."

We decided to ask them if they might consider a direct airline flight to Vermont. Except, this time, I would fly to Florida and drive their packed car and dog, Lady, to Vermont and fly back to El Paso.

Barbara called them with the proposal.

"To be honest," my mom said, "your father and I talked and decided to forgo our usual trip this year."

I was caught completely off guard. This was the first time my mother ever suggested not spending the summer at the Luck camp.

Within two months, my mother was admitted to St. Joseph's Hospital in Port Charlotte, Florida. She complained of an intense shooting pain in her leg with difficulty breathing. Immediately, I flew to Florida to be with her and support my father. At that point, he was struggling to remember exactly how to get to and from the hospital.

My mother lay in the hospital and slowly declined over several days with no particular diagnosis. Doctors suggested my mother had numerous cascading health issues. Multiple organ systems were collapsing like dominoes. I was gravely concerned with the veiled looks and coded words used by hospital professionals to describe diminished outcomes. From their reports, my mother's health trajectory looked perilous. I was heartbroken. My mother was not likely to be going home. Now, I had some difficult decisions to make. If my mother died, it would be catastrophic. I contemplated the painful possibility of how my father would cope without Mary.

It was important for me to hold my emotions in check for my father. We talked about Mary's steady decline without ever mentioning the possibility of her death. However, I sensed my father knew Mary would not pull through. Carefully, we began to talk about what might happen if Mom died. I suspected what my father might say, but I wanted to hear what he was thinking and feeling. The discussion helped us both prepare for our next chapter together.

I stayed with my mother until the end.

She died on May 11, 1993, when she was 81. I was irreparably cleaved from my mother, whose single goal had been my happiness. I was crushed, the burden unbearable. My father was lost and in some stage of denial. He couldn't believe she simply was gone.

A funeral needed to be planned. I was in Florida, and Barbara was in El Paso, Texas. The plan was to fly to Burlington, Vermont, with my father and wait for Mary's body to be transported there for a funeral with family and friends. Barbara and Jonathan would arrive from Texas, while Holly and Sean would come from Massachusetts.

Soon, the Ready Funeral home visiting hours brought family and friends together. A Catholic Mass was celebrated at St. Thomas Church in Underhill near Mary's birthplace.

I tearfully choked on my feelings as I started my eulogy,

Thank you for being here today and for all your kindness, remembrances, and thoughtfulness on behalf of our mother.

She was born on Saturday at 5:30 p.m. eighty-one years ago on the Leddy/Marlow farm less than a mile from here and attended this church.

We gather today to remember, to cherish, to be sad together, but most importantly, to celebrate her life. You knew my mother in many roles. My two sisters, Nancy and Rosemary, and I called her 'Mom.' But she was also a wife and my father's best friend for over fifty-seven years. She was an aunt, a grandmother, a sister, a niece, a colleague, a Bridge partner who could make faces to telegraph any good hand, and 'Mrs. Luck' to all her high school students.

Mom would have been thrilled you came today. She so loved each of you and spoke of you often, in detail. You all know Mary never forgot anything. But today, my mother takes on a new role. She's in heaven with her parents, John T. Leddy and Anna Marlow, her brother, Bernard, and a baby brother who died in infancy. Most importantly, she's also in heaven with her daughter, our sister Rosemary, who died decades ago from cystic fibrosis. Rosemary's been waiting a long time for my mother's hugs and love.

All of Mary's grandchildren were present. My children selected readings and Sean spoke of frequent humorous interactions with his grandmother. He knew from her tone of voice when she called, "Sean...eee" he was about to receive an assignment or chore she needed performed. He also shared fond memories of Grandma Luck's special camp lunches and picnics prepared for hikes with her insistence they pack a thermos of chocolate milk, which usually curdled way too soon.

A reception was held nearby at the Underhill Town Hall, a hundred yards from the one-room schoolhouse where Mary attended school as a child. Her life had come full circle. This was a heart-wrenching time for all of us. Most young children want to believe their parents and grandparents will always be with them. Then, suddenly, one day, they're not. I decided my mother's death would hurt as much as it was worth. It was excruciating.

After the funeral I returned with Bill to Florida while Barbara and Jonathan flew back to El Paso. Unfortunately, their beloved elderly dog, Lady, passed away soon after. With no reason for Dad to remain in Florida, we decided to settle him close to us in El Paso at an independent living residence. I began the difficult and painful task of preparing my parents' Florida home for sale. Each item in the household held a memory, something to hold and remember, which easily transported me to another place and time.

In El Paso, we moved Dad to a ground-floor three-room apartment with an alcove for reading or television viewing plus an outdoor terrace. The place was comfortably furnished with familiar household items from Florida. For my father, it was a new life in a different place without Mary and his dog.

Fortunately, the downsizing lessened the complexity of Bill's life and made it manageable. All his meals and services were provided, so there were few worries. There were new faces and friends, all in the same circumstances, to be discovered. The staff at the retirement community were sympathetic, kind and knew of all his recent losses. They made a special effort to support him as he adjusted to his new surroundings.

My father's Florida driver's license was long gone, but this tiny detail apparently wasn't a deterrent. After he settled into his new apartment, Bill decided he needed a car. Unannounced, he took a cab to a used car lot ten miles across the city. How he found the place, much less managed to pull off such a stunt, heaven only knows.

The next day, we visited my father for an evening dinner together. As we sat for a few moments on his terrace, he gushed, "How do you like my new car?"

Surprised, I quickly glanced at my father and then over the terrace retaining wall. "What new car? You can't drive. What are you talking about?" I hoped my father was pulling my leg. I should have known better.

He gestured, "See that beige-colored car by the tree? It's mine."

I said, "You mean the one with the cracked windshield?"

"Yup!"

I looked at my father's new acquisition. It was a sad-looking jalopy. The following day, Barbara and I took Bill's jalopy back to the salesman to get his money back.

Regrettably, Bill's mental condition continued to deteriorate. Over time, he stopped asking about his Florida home, Mary, and his dog Lady.

Time Heals All Wounds

~ 6 ~

INFORMATION OVERLOAD

Recent family traumas caused me to seriously consider revisiting the topic of my biological parents.

I guessed they must be in their mid-sixties, if they were still alive. For the first time in thirty years, I seriously mused about how I might search for them. How would I start and where would I look?

My search was more than curiosity. As I got older, I realized my biological family history was important to me and my children. What health issues might my biological parents and relatives wrestled with? Did some family members have diabetes? Did others have chronic heart disease or poor mobility? On a more personal level, I was interested in what kind of people they were. Did they have a sense of humor? What talents, achievements, characteristics, and personalities did they have? How did they live their lives? Was I like them in any way? What would it be like to meet them?

"How would you feel if I finally began the search for my biological parents?" I asked Barbara over dinner one night.

She paused for just a moment. "Sorry, that caught me off guard. I thought you'd decided it wasn't necessary."

"That's true, but you know, with Mom's death and Dad's declining health, it might be the right time. I'm feeling more and more an urgent curiosity. Just as importantly, finding information about them could provide much-needed information about my family health history."

"I agree. I'm happy to support your journey. We are all curious, too."

With Barbara's encouragement and parallel enthusiasm, I initiated a search for my birth mother. I knew it would be an arduous process with results that were not guaranteed. So, I started with what I knew. According to my birth certificate, I was born at the Bishop DeGoesbriand Hospital in Burlington, Vermont, on March 26, 1947. Maybe that would be a good place to start.

I wrote letters of inquiry to the Vermont Catholic Charities, the Probate Court of Chittenden County, and the State of Vermont Department of Social and Rehabilitation Services requesting any details or information about my adoption.

On February 11th, 1993, I received my first reply from the Probate Court:

In Vermont, we have a disclosure law, which maintains that all adoption records are confidential and secret, and only identifying information can be issued after receiving written consent from the adoptee and the biological parents and notifying the adoptive parents about a twenty-five-dollar fee. The identity of your natural father was never disclosed, and your natural mother has not contacted this office. As a consequence, we have no consent from her and can do nothing until such consent is received.

What we can tell you is you were a normal baby without giving any medical information. Your father was supposed to be of Scotch-Irish descent, and he would be sixty-nine at this time. Your mother was of German-English descent and described as healthy, physically attractive, and of high normal intelligence.

This was the first puzzle piece of the missing part of my life. I was excited to learn a few insights about my birth with tantalizing tips about my biological background. This was exciting, and it made me want to learn more. I was hooked.

A month later, I received another reply, this time from the Department of Social and Rehabilitation Services. Their response surprised me. The department shared an unusual volume of information without restrictions. My early life was chronicled in a case file.

Dear Mr. Luck,

You were born on March 26, 1947, at the DeGoesbriand Hospital in Burlington, Vermont, now a part of the University of Vermont Medical Center. You remained in the hospital nursery for a month after your birth and were then transferred to the Saint Joseph's Orphanage and Asylum. You were placed with Bill and Mary Luck on May 27, 1947.

Your birth mother was born in 1927 in New York State, an only child. She is of German/English descent. She was raised by her mother and stepfather after her parents divorced when she was five years of age. She is a high school graduate and a healthy, athletic type. Before her marriage, she was employed in an office, where she was considered an able and responsible employee. She married her high school boyfriend.

They had been engaged previously, but she broke the engagement when she found out he was seeing other women. That's when she met your birth father. At the time of their marriage, she was pregnant with you. Her husband was not your father. Her husband arranged for her to be placed at the hospital several months prior to your birth for social protection and with a plan of adoption for you.

Your birth father was born in New Jersey in 1922. He was the oldest of six children of Scotch-Irish descent. He was employed at a summer resort owned by your birth mother's family. He came to know your birth mother there, and they enjoyed such activities as swimming and dancing together. Although he did know your mother was pregnant, he apparently did not know she had given birth. She simply never told him.

I was flabbergasted. The detailed confidential insights seemed too good to be true. It was an overwhelming amount of information to digest after going so long without any knowledge at all. I surmised some dedicated social worker must have spent a lot of time with my birth mother compiling an extensive background file, maybe for this very situation. My birth mother must have told her everything, and the social worker wrote it all down. As I read and reread the letter, I began forming a mental picture of what my birth parents might be like. The Vermont Department recommended a "deeper" search if I wanted more answers. Better results would require a knowledgeable "adoption search specialist," a seasoned sleuth to make discreet inquiries.

With good fortune, I was given the name of a woman named Beth Thomas from St. Albans, Vermont. She was an adoption specialist and fellow adoptee with an enviable track record of helping people find long-lost birth parents. Beth's business plan was simple: she was good at finding people. She donated her time with a minimal fee for personal expenses such as telephone, gas, and administrative fees. This was more a labor of love for her than a profession.

When I spoke to Beth, she said, "The cost would probably be less than a few hundred dollars, but the search might take a while."

Laughing, I mentioned, "After forty-four years, there's no big rush."

I armed Beth with all the information furnished by the Vermont agencies regarding the orphanage and my adoption. She said the most important piece of information was "when and where" I was born. She was able to quickly narrow the search to a small number of possibilities. How many male babies were delivered at the Bishop DeGoesbriand Hospital on March 26, 1947? Who were the mothers? How many matched some of the details from the Vermont Department's letter?

Beth promised that she would call me only when she had a lead. Weeks passed with no news. I wondered why but realized I was just being impatient. I thought back to when I was fifteen and first saw the word "adopted" by my name. Each adoption has its unique trajectory of secrets and layers of the unknown. Everything was in the hands of fate.

Fortunately, Beth had a friend at the Bishop DeGoesbriand Hospital who had access to old birth records. Birth registrations from the 1940s were printed on 5 X 7 cards stored in sealed boxes. Some of the details had been redacted but, when held to the light, revealed critical information. Soon, Beth's hospital source called to report good news. Only one woman gave birth to a boy on March 26, 1947. Her name was Rita June Maloney and her address, at that time, was Rutland, Vermont.

Beth's next step was to conduct an online search for her in Rutland. Even after more than four decades she hoped Rita might still live there. It was a long shot, but Beth was hopeful. She looked at the Rutland city tax records, which revealed no one named Rita Maloney. The next step was a search for an individual named Rita, about sixty-five years old, with a possible different last name.

Beth called with an update. "Good news! I found twenty-two individuals named Rita and only one with the middle name June. She had divorced and remarried. She was now Rita June Mills. So, the next step for me is to write her a letter and see if she will respond. Are you comfortable with that?" Beth asked.

For a moment, I was silent as I tried to process this new information. My birth mother's name was Rita June Mills! I couldn't believe we were getting close. "Yes, Beth, of course," I blurted out. "Let's see what happens."

Beth wrote a letter to Rita that was marked confidential, and her goal was two-fold. First, she wanted to verify Rita was the woman who gave birth in 1947. Second, it was important to find out if she had any interest in any form of contact or relationship with the baby that she gave up over four decades earlier.

November 17, 1993:
Dear Mrs. Mills,
I'm writing concerning a personal, confidential, and important issue. I have been asked to be a liaison for someone searching for his birth mother.

My client's name is Michael. He was born on March 26, 1947, at the Bishop DeGoesbriand Hospital in Burlington, Vermont. He knows his last name at birth was Maloney. If these facts are a part of your history, I would like to communicate with you in strictest confidence. My client doesn't want to cause heartache or harm and doesn't need or want anything from you. He would like some answers about his biological heritage, birth, and more if you're willing. It can all be handled by mail and through me if you would prefer to keep everything secret and confidential.

I would appreciate a response from you one way or the other. If we have contacted the wrong person, I will continue to search.

Please respond in confidence to my mail address below. I anxiously await a response.

Sincerely,
Beth Thomas
Adoption Search Specialist

On Saturday, November 20, 1993, Beth called to tell me she received a response from Rita. She was pleased to relay the exciting news she had uncovered.

"Congratulations, Michael," she said. "I have some good news for you. I found your birth mother. Fortunately, I was able to determine your mother hadn't gone far. She was still living in Rutland, Vermont, but under a different last name. She had remarried since her divorce from her first husband. I sent your mother a letter in total confidence and described the details of your birth. She wrote back and confirmed all the facts and dates were accurate. Most importantly, she's thrilled you found her and is willing to communicate with you.

You were the only child she ever had. She said when you're ready, you can call her."

That was a lot of information to digest all at once. I was my mother's only child. This unveiling frightened and excited me at the same time. This seemed like a lot happening, and I hadn't really expected that Beth would find anything, much less promising news. Maybe it was my way of keeping my hopes in-check.

Stunned by Beth's announcement, I realized I had been foolish to think simple biological information might be retrieved and nothing else. Now, a lot more things might quickly unravel.

Beth continued, "Your mother's name is Rita June Mills. She was married to Tom Maloney for seven years and then divorced. He died a long time ago. Much later in her life, she married Edward Mills, Jr. Apparently, he does not know of your existence. Rita never told him. So, she wants you to know that if the two of you have an open dialogue, she will have to tell her husband. She suggested she wasn't sure how the announcement would affect their marriage. The hint was things could be tense for a while. She hopes you understand her predicament. Her heart is aching.

When you were born, the hospital staff whisked you away before she could see you. She never thought she'd know or see you ever again. Since your birth, she has lived each day with the knowledge she tragically gave away a piece of herself. The fact that Rita's mother sent her a Mother's Day card every year didn't help.

"If you are ready, here is your mother's telephone number...... I have done my part. The rest is up to you. Please give me a call if there are any complications or problems connecting with your mother. If I can be of further assistance, I am happy to do so. Let me know how this all works out. I am so happy for you."

I caught my breath. My head spun, and my response was spirited.

"Beth, I cannot thank you enough for this moment. Yes, I will call her. I need some time to collect myself. This is all good news and more than I expected. I need to integrate the implications. The next step will be momentous. What a great job you have done. Thank you again for all your hard work. You have been marvelous and made me so happy. I will always be eternally grateful and will let you know what happens."

I hung up the phone and tried to process the news. A surprising river of tears erupted. I stared at my birth mother's phone number.

She was ten digits away. Did I really want to open the door? Once I did, there would be no turning back. I knew that one call would alter all our lives.

In the midst of my angst, Barbara entered the room.

"I heard the phone ring; who called?"

When she saw my face, she must have sensed something terrible had happened. I had tears streaking across my face, and I was shaking.

I said, "It was Beth. She told me she had found my birth mother and confirmed all the details. The best part is my birth mother has agreed to have contact with me and wants me to call her. Her name is Rita June Mills, and she lives in Rutland, Vermont, but I can't call her right now. I need to collect myself. This is all overwhelming." My voice trembled as I paused to catch my breath.

Barbara said, "My God, how amazing and wonderful! What a huge surprise! How are you feeling? When are you going to call her?"

I raised both my hands, "I don't know. I need time to think. I need to rehearse. What do I say, 'Hi, Mom, it's been a while?' or 'Hello, Mrs. Mills, this is your son Michael?' or 'Hey, Rita, how ya doing?' If I call her, I should probably do it alone."

Barbara gave me a long, tender hug and kiss. She whispered quietly, "This is the moment I know you have been waiting and hoping for. I love you. I'm sure everything will be all right. I'm going to take Jonathan to run some errands. We will be back in a few hours."

~ 7 ~

THE CONVERSATION

I dialed my birth mother's telephone number.

In a moment, I would hear her voice for the first time. I had rehearsed how to begin the conversation, but I wondered what her voice would sound like. How would she react to my voice? What would she tell me? What would she ask? I thought Rita must be nervous, too. She was probably already wondering what was taking me so long to call.

Her phone rang three times, and then a tentative but enthusiastic voice answered, "Hello, Rita Mills!"

I softly said, "Hello, this is Michael. It's good to hear your voice."

There was a long, long silence. No one spoke. It became clear that we were both sobbing, too emotional to speak.

After several moments, Rita spoke first. "I'm so sorry. Please forgive me. I didn't expect to be so overwhelmed. I do hope you understand."

I collected myself and sputtered, "No need to apologize. I'm crying, too! It's okay. We can take our time. The reason I didn't call you right away was I simply couldn't. If I had called, no sound would have come out of my mouth. So, don't apologize for your emotions; I feel the same."

We both laughed with great relief. With the tension lifted, we began a long conversation. It lasted more than two hours and flowed naturally as if we had just spoken a week ago.

Rita's voice had a reedy growl, not in a threatening manner, more like a movie starlet affected by too many gin martinis and cigarettes. The banter was free and easy, with as many questions as there were answers. The conversation roamed without sequence or order. As people or places popped into our heads, the conversation jumped around like a field full of jackrabbits. There were moments when I wasn't sure if the two of us were talking simply because neither one of us wanted to hang up. It was the sheer joy of hearing each other's voices.

We agreed we would write to each other and send photos as soon as possible. With our lives in El Paso, Texas, and Rita in Rutland, Vermont, a quick meeting was not in the cards. The U.S. postal service and phone calls would have to suffice for the moment. It was too early to devise a long-range plan, so we reluctantly said "goodbye" to each other and promised to talk again soon.

I was euphoric. Rita sounded like a nice person. The sort of woman I imagined who might give birth to someone like me. The phone call was a sudden confirmation of our shared past. It would forever change the fit and feel of everything.

Not long after I hung up the phone, Barbara and Jonathan returned home.

"Did you call your mother?" Barbara asked.

"Yes, it was a surreal experience. It was filled with too many emotions. I'm not even sure what we talked about. It's good you weren't here. We rambled on and on as if time didn't matter."

Barbara seemed pleased and relieved. This was a giant first step, and it was a success. "What did you talk about? What did she say? Did the two of you decide what should happen next?"

I did my best to relay the highlights of the conversation, including that we agreed to write and exchange photos to get to know each other. We also agreed it would be quite nice to select a time and place to meet, perhaps in the spring.

My next thought was, should I share this important news with my father, Bill? Out of deep respect and love for my adoptive parents, I never asked about my adoption. Sharing news about finding Rita, I sensed, would not be in my father's best interest. With all of my father's recent losses, this piece of news might be too much. He would probably be supportive, but he might also wonder why I felt a desire to search in the first place. Clearly, secrets had been kept for a reason, and now probably wasn't the best time to reveal all of them.

Weighing the dramatic news about my birth mother, I wondered how others would feel and react. Sharing the news of a "new" biological grandmother with my three children could be traumatic. All they knew growing up were Grandma and Grandpa Luck and Grandparents Ward and Evelyn Benzie, plus (step)grandparents Carroll and Mary Wilson.

So, the news of Rita's existence could be bewildering, and perhaps, an unwanted displacement. In a flash, I decided to slow things down. Although the proverbial "cat was now peeking out of the bag," it didn't mean the cat had to rush out and knock everything over.

***

Hurriedly, I assembled several photos, my résumé, which seemed wholly inadequate, but it was descriptive in a holistic way as well as other family details and sent it all off to Rita.

November 24, 1993

Dear Rita,

It was wonderful to talk with you on the telephone. It was more than wonderful, but I am still unable to fully appreciate this new aspect of my life. I was laughing after our phone call because you were worrying about the phone bill. I was thinking, after forty-five years, who cares?

We have so much to catch up on and so much time to get to know one another, it is hard to know where to begin. Enclosed are my professional résumé, selected photos, and written materials relating to my life and family going back to when I was a baby. They are yours to keep. I look forward to another phone call after we have exchanged some family information. I know we will each have a ton of questions.

Naturally, I can't wait to see you and want to repeat my suggestion that you and your husband, Eddie, might come to El Paso, Texas, this winter if you can. I will send you plane tickets. I am sorry we live so far away.

I think the chance to be together for a few days would be a great way to get acquainted. It would also be terrific to see your mother, Ethyl (my grandmother), for the first time if she would like to do so. At some point, we will make a special trip to Vermont with great joy.

I can't wait to hear from you!!

Love,

Michael

P.S. Have a great Thanksgiving. I know mine will be the best ever!

The letters crossed in the mail. Rita wrote,

November 28, 1993

Dear Michael and Family,

Your Federal Express package arrived. You are so good-looking! To a mother, you're beautiful, but best, I just know it in my heart. Your family is so lovely. You have to be full of pride. I caress your pictures each night before bed.

While going through the material you sent, I cried, laughed, and read and reread. It's so overwhelming. I feel like I'll never remember it all. Your achievements are so wonderful and must have taken much effort and long hours of dedication. Barbara can be proud of all you have accomplished together! She must have put in endless hours to support the family, have her own career, and support your endeavors.

I am sending you an angel for your Christmas tree. It expresses my feelings about two miracles this year: the birth of the Christ child and my own miracle, Michael.

Love and best wishes,
Rita and Ed

In twenty-four hours, a package from Rita also arrived. I was excited. I stared at the large manila envelope, which I knew would contain promising revelations. There was no perfect place to start, so Rita poured out her heart:

To my son Michael and his precious family,
I've always held to the belief you pay for your happiness with heartaches. If this analogy can be believed, then my heartaches of long ago were of such enormity it's truly proportional to the happiness I am feeling now. I've had twenty-six happy years with my wonderful husband Ed and now find you are alive and have been searching for me. My heart is bursting and it can never exceed such immense feeling.

So many years have passed, and at age sixty-five, I realize the sand is running out. It felt like an insurmountable task to absorb everything I want to experience, with only a few years to do it in. Incredibly, I feel I want to hold you near and rock you in my arms so I might recapture forty-five years, but I know this is ridiculous.

I will never be able to have your parents know how much I love them for loving you in my place. They are your true parents, as they nourished you and shared all of your hopes and dreams.

Rita then described her sad marriage to her first husband, Tom Maloney:

My eight years married to Tom were most unhappy as he drank heavily and was a heartache to his family and to me. I feel his duty in the Marine Corps in the South Pacific changed him. He began dating me when I was fifteen, a freshman in high school. He already graduated. Because of his family's comfortable background, Tom traveled with an exciting crowd, which, to a fifteen-year-old, was fantastic.

When Tom joined the Marines, my mother's second husband, Alexander Stapchuk (Uncle to Sandra Dee, the movie star), worked winters (when the family's summer resort closed for the season) on the shipping docks of New York. He found out Tom was getting leaves from the Army but not coming to see me. When my stepfather told me, it broke my heart. I told Tom our relationship was over and that I would date others. His family begged me to give him a second chance, as he was young and "sowing his wild oats." I declined."

As the days became months, letters between us flew back and forth. Receiving and comprehending so much historical information was a herculean task. Every aspect of my life had to be rebooted. Each piece required a new self-perspective. My life seemed like a single deck of cards constantly being reshuffled with another deck to integrate the "two" into one. Each additional piece of news changed my perceptions of what I thought I knew and raised more questions.

In early January, Barbara jumped into the correspondence circle with a heartfelt letter to Rita, which read in part:

January 2, 1994
Dear Rita and Ed,
I have been thinking about you over the holidays and thought I would put some character behind Michael's words.

Yes, it is quite something to know you and Michael have found one another. It was interesting how, throughout the process of searching for you, I kept asking Michael how he felt. He remained objective until he received the incredible Sunday phone call when he told me Beth Thomas had called and you were waiting for his call. I started to cry. Then we cried together. What a thrill to find you alive and well and living with your beloved Ed. It was heart-wrenching as a mother to know Michael was your only child and he was given up for adoption. And then, the circumstances of your life with Tom Maloney made it even more overwhelming to absorb. However, you have been so generous with us, filling us in on so many details of your life and family history. Thank you.

I thought I would speak to both of you, but with Ed in mind since I find myself in the counterpart position as he does. Michael has held each picture and piece of correspondence privately. He does not let me read his letters to you right away and keeps the ones he writes to you personal. I sometimes wonder what outrageous stuff he is saying. All of this, of course, creates a sense of being left out, when most other areas of our life together we fully share. It is as if Michael has a "lover" or, indeed, has another woman in his life. Although I understand and embrace the truth, the actuality doesn't diminish the feelings of being a bit left out.

At first, I wondered why I was feeling envious when, in fact, I was feeling overwhelmingly joyous that we connected with you, Rita. As it turned out, it was these feelings of their being another "lover" that was bothering me. In time, I have come to understand these feelings and Michael and I have talked about them, wondering if Ed might be having some of the same feelings. For you, Ed, after all these years, to have someone as your wife's son appear must be quite a bombshell! I, at least, was aware from the time I met Michael he was adopted, and our conversation revolved around the topic periodically over the years.

So, what does all this mean? To me it means we might consider finding a way so we can move forward in getting to know both of you and your family so the feelings are inclusive rather than exclusive. I noted you wish to meet Michael alone first. I wholly respect whatever it is you and Michael decide. However, may I suggest that Michael and his children, along with me, are eager to meet you? Sean and Holly, in Boston, and eventually Jonathan (we haven't told him yet because his grandfather was going to be here over Christmas) would like to meet you. I happen to also be keen on meeting your mother since she is likely to know the joy of such beautiful great-grandchildren, especially in her twilight years.

So, what can we do about this?

Best wishes to you both, and we look forward to meeting you.

Love,

Barbara

Rita was also facing a similar struggle. How to share the news she had a son.

Rita wrote:

January 8, 1994
Dear Barbara,
You have made me so happy with your letter. There was a scary feeling inside me, you might be wishing this was not happening. You are quite perceptive, during the holidays my husband Ed was especially quiet, not a part of the holiday spirit. I asked him more than once, if anything was bothering him and he would reply, "No." I even asked him if his lack of spirit had to do with my son and he still replied, "No."

It was when I read your letter to him he admitted he knew how you felt. There has always been just the two of us, and I think he is all torn up inside, not knowing what is in the future. He has always been present when I call family members to tell them about Michael, and he feels helpless watching me cry. It upset him to see me so upset. My mother was the only family member who knew about my baby. Telling her, I was afraid how much of a shock it might be for her, even knowing she would share my joy. After I told her my son had found me, she called every day. She was worrying about me!

Barbara, my only reason for wanting to see Michael alone was because I may fall apart. I constantly try to have thoughts that might help me have better control of myself. I cry in order to make myself feel the complete happiness of it all and not the terrible loss of forty-five years. There is no way to ever begin to describe the traumatic loss. I have this wonderful happening, to have my son love me enough to find me and want me to be a part of his life. It makes me love him even more than I thought possible. Nothing can ever replace the years lost; what a tragedy it was. As a mother, you know.

I rationalize Mother and Father Luck loved Michael dearly and gave him a wonderful education, I would have been unable to do. Through his education he met you. I cannot go back and do things differently. How could I have known I would never have another child after Michael?

Barbara, I love you even though I have never met you because you have so much love for Michael, your children, and, I hope, even for me. You have taken my fears away at meeting all of you and discovering you all care. It will all work out for us, I'm sure. God has gotten us this far, so we better have faith that He will make all the pieces fall into place. Someday, we will probably look back on all our apprehension and laugh. One thing for sure is we will never forget the 1993 holidays!

Ed and I are both looking forward to seeing you all. Your idea is great. I will check out available condos and let you know quickly.

Thank you for taking the time to write and for your thoughtfulness.
Love,
Rita June

Finally, we made plans for a spring meeting. It would be the first meeting for everyone in Rita's hometown. We would fly from Texas to Vermont. Sean and Holly would travel from Massachusetts, and we would all intersect at a convenient spot to find our way to Rita's home. Sean, twenty-seven years old and a recent graduate from Worcester Polytechnic Institute, had just started his first job at Cognex Corporation, an early inventor of machines to read "bar codes." Holly, twenty-three years old, a recent graduate of Boston's Northeastern University, was in the early throes of establishing an elementary school teacher career.

Rita was ecstatic about meeting everyone. She had told her mother, Ethyl, and siblings, George and Terry, about the proposed meeting with me and my family. They were all invited. Rita excitedly put pen to paper:

January 23, 1994
Dear Barbara and Michael,
Thank you for making plans to come to Rutland. I have secured a Barley Hills condo for your visit. It will be comfortable for you with plenty

of bedrooms. It has 2½ baths, two double beds, two bunk beds, and two twin beds.

I can't wait to see all the rest of the family (my grandchildren). Just saying it and seeing it on paper is unbelievable. I'm so grateful they want to see me. I feel so lucky and so fortunate as if there aren't words adequate enough for how I feel. I'm scared, even though I am so happy. I imagine, suppose, they don't like me and are disappointed or expect someone perfect. I don't even know how to describe myself. Ed says I'm a perfectionist, but I say I just take pride in anything I do. Doing it the best I can with what I have to work with. I'm outgoing, kind-hearted, and loyal. I have a temper but try not to lose my cool if I can help it. I like to be around people but like time alone, too.

I am taking every day slow with my husband. He has had a lot to absorb. He hasn't talked about this new chapter in our lives, so I don't know what he's feeling. Ed and I usually have great conversations. He is now a lot more reserved. In the meantime, I am cooking up a storm so we will have hardly any cooking to do when you're here.

Love you all,
Rita and Ed

Rita wrote letters to her grandchildren so they would get to know her and feel warmly welcomed. Her first letter was to her youngest grandchild, Jonathan:

February 15, 1994
Dear Jonathan,
Soon we will meet, and you will have so much to share which I'll be interested in. I'm going to be nervous and scared to meet you, so I hope you will help me. I didn't know I was your grandmother until your father located me. So, I'm new at this "being a grandmother."
I'm going to be different from what you believe I'll be like, at least I think so. I love movies and taping movies with the VCR. I also occasionally like to listen to a scanner for local accidents and fires. I love to shop, eat

lunch, and collect stamps. I hate to throw anything away so my home is bulging at the seams.

I understand you play the piano. I hope to hear you play someday. Your great-great-grandmother's family all played musical instruments: the harp, piano, banjo, violin, and guitar. Your great-grandmother played the piano and organ but not classical. She hasn't played in many years as she is blind and almost ninety. She was a terrific lady in her younger years when people were wearing long clinging gowns that swirled at their knees when they danced in popular clubs. Jimmy Durante played a lot where she went. The family owned a summer resort where generations of families stayed for vacations. Your great-grandmother's father (Jennings) was the most wonderful grandfather to all of us children. We had ice-skating parties on a large pond nearby with bonfires at night to warm our feet. We had sleigh rides and hayrides, and he always got us out of trouble when we did something devilish (which was often).

I'll be anxious to see you and hope you will like Rutland. We are only ten miles from the Killington ski area. Pico Peak is even nearer. When you're here I want you to see a sculpture which artist Patrick Farrow gave to the city. Farrow's mother is Maureen O'Sullivan, the movie star (she played "Jane" in all the Tarzan movies). The sculpture is called "Dog on a Leash."

In the meantime, I will continue to feed the squirrels in our backyard. They are hard to tell apart but we have started to name them. The fattest one we call "Numb Nuts." He (I guess?) along with the others are hard to keep out of the bird feeders. They are little rascals.

Until we meet, I send you my love and will be fidgeting when you arrive.
Good luck in your concert. Wish I could be there.
Love you,
Grandmother Mills

~ 8 ~

FULL CIRCLE

Rita was ready and wanted to look her best for my arrival.

She had more outfits laid out on her bed to wear than most shops have in their inventory. She asked herself, "Should I wear summer pink or light green? Perhaps a pale yellow would be better?" She tried on all the outfits, mixed and matched them with appropriate jewelry and shoes, and finally arrived at a suitable ensemble. Peach! Her pleated slacks with cuffs fell perfectly in a break over her shoes with medium solid heels. The blouse, a swirl of soft pastel colors, was topped off with a bright silk jacket as a contrast to the rest of her outfit. She looked stunning. Rita also dressed husband Eddie so he would also be presentable. She laid out his clothes: slacks, a dress shirt, and a complementary sport coat, in case the moment called for such formality. As usual, it was the only choice Eddie had to make.

By March 7, 1994, everyone in Rutland knew we were coming.

As we neared the house, I gazed at the sixty-five-year-old woman standing on her front porch. I had long wrestled with what this moment might be like. Elated at the prospect of meeting my biological mother, I still felt a twinge of disloyalty to my adoptive parents. I had felt the same way when I started my search. My Catholic upbringing made me wish I had rosary beads to make an act of contrition.

On that cold, overcast day, Rita waved excitedly. We all waved, too. Without warning, she suddenly flew off the porch and raced across the lawn like a thoroughbred. She met me halfway, and we embraced tenderly as tears flowed. It felt as if I were holding a long-lost treasure. Time stood still. The moment signaled a new future.

The spell broke when Rita looked over my shoulder and said, "Barbara and the grandchildren!" I watched in amazement as Rita greeted Barbara and the children with warm embraces. The hugs were continuous and interrupted with quick looks at each other, then more hugs again and again. The loving greeting was filled with nervous laughter. It all seemed surreal to be affectionate with someone known by phone calls, photos, and letters. Despite all the expressions of joy, we were still strangers.

When hugs and kisses concluded, Eddie appeared on the porch like a "second act." He welcomed everyone inside. Rita snapped out of her ethereal moment and escorted her new family inside her home for refreshments.

While staring at each other, the usual banter ensued, "How was the trip and the traffic? Did you find our house okay?"

***

Later, at the Rutland South Street Restaurant, words and stories continued to flow without judgment. The whirlwind of my emotions peaked as I quietly assessed how this new relationship might work. Rita appeared to be the same sweet woman I had corresponded with during the past several months. I still struggled to imagine Rita as my "birth mother," even though she was.

The next morning, over breakfast, we all spoke with wonder about what had happened the day before. Meeting Rita and Eddie had been a strange experience. Rita was a wonderful lady, but it was also awkward for the children. I could sense they weren't quite ready to think of her as "Dad's mother" or "Grandma Rita" just yet.

We poured over stacks of Rita's photo albums to help recapture her past and perhaps create an inclusive future. Naturally, each picture evoked an exchange of questions. "Where did Rita grow up?

What kinds of things did she most enjoy?" The pictures helped us get to know one another.

***

I had a forty-six-year loving memory of my adoptive mother, Mary Luck, and Rita was obviously quite different. She wasn't different in a bad way; she just didn't seem like my mother. I wrestled with how to reconcile my mixed feelings about what I had imagined her to be like and how she actually was. It wasn't a comparison, but the process of getting to know one another would take time.

The next day, Rita arrived at the condo where we were staying with lunch for the day's big event. She confessed she hardly slept. Within thirty minutes, there was a knock on the condo door. Bursting with pride, Rita warmly greeted her mother, Ethyl, George, and his wife, Clara, as they arrived from East Durham, New York. Rita's sister, Terry, lived in Virginia and was unable to come. Expectations were high. There was an emotional round of introductions and hugs.

My new grandmother, Ethyl, quickly wrapped me in a long, warm embrace and whispered, "I always hoped someday you'd find your way home. It's so good to finally see you and to give you a hug and kiss. My heart has ached, and I've missed you, knowing what Rita endured. I know Rita has always yearned for a chance to love you. You've always been in my thoughts and heart. This is a moment I'll remember forever."

Ethyl then turned to Barbara and her great-grandchildren to greet them. Uncle George reached out to shake my hand. We hugged each other instead. There was an abundance of warmth and amazement. Photos were taken, videos recorded, and stories were told as everyone sat around a big table explaining and asking questions. Each tried to discover threads of affinity, plumbing the depths of similarities, hobbies, education, interests, and passions. It helped establish greater familiarity and a family bond.

Rita beamed with joy. Elated that most of her family was able to meet me, Barbara, and our family, the afternoon passed quickly.

Ethyl, George, and his wife, Clara, eventually said goodbye and returned to East Durham. Heartfelt tears were on display with promises of another family gathering. The moment was fraught with high emotion and memories not soon forgotten.

The next morning, we packed for our own departure. Rita was visibly tense as we loaded our suitcases. She seemed confronted with the reality of having to say goodbye to me again after forty-five years. Even Eddie had warmed up a bit as he realized these new people in Rita's life appeared somewhat normal and were not likely to meddle in his life. It appeared that Eddie was relieved we weren't trying to steal Rita with ulterior motives.

With tears flowing, Rita gave us all a brave smile as we waved goodbye out the car window. She had successfully hugged and kissed her only child for the first time in a half-century. She could now say she was a mother, mother-in-law, and grandmother.

***

When we arrived home in El Paso, I received a letter from Rita. She must have written as soon as we departed.

March 10, 1993
Dear Michael, Barbara, and Jonathan,
After you drove away, I felt such an enormous emptiness. Part of my heart went with you. There are no words to express how much I love all of you. You have given me such a beautiful family. Anyone would be so puffed up with pride they would be bursting.

I love you, Michael. You are all and more than any mother could ever ask for. And, Barbara, you are so loving and good to me. I shall never forget all you did. Sean, Holly, and Jonathan are a joy, talented, and smart as a whip. They are wonderful. I want to thank all of you again for spending time with me. Please thank Jonathan for being so generous to play the piano for us at South Station restaurant. What handsome and beautiful grandchildren!

All of you went through much effort and expense to come to see me and I will love you forever for it. Young people today are so caught up in "doing their own thing" I think your family was terrific to have given me this long weekend. I shall never forget.

The laughable part of a "first meeting" with relatives is everyone spilling out our idiosyncrasies. Now it's behind us. It's a sixty-five-year spread of ages with a lot of experience and hopefully some wisdom.

I want you to always be proud that I'm your mother, and I hope to do all I can to be the best mother. The pictures captured poignant moments. The photos of my mother, Ethyl, are unbelievable for her age. I know she was so happy she lived to meet all of you. Her dream, to see all of you before she died, came true.

At least now I've seen you, I know you are real, so only half of me is here in Vermont and the other half is with you. I have to close this letter and get it off to you. I keep crying for joy. I need to stop so this letter can be sent. Please forgive the delay.

All my love,

Mother Rita June and Ed

P.S. Ed has been mushy and loving, so I think he is coming to rest with all these new happenings. He told me I have a wonderful family. Ed's mother, Betty, said so, too.

Rita's brother, George, also sent a letter:

March 12, 1993

Dear Barbara, Michael, and Jonathan,

I've (We've) been thinking a lot since I met your family. What a God-given gift to have a son return to a mother's life with such joy and love.

Only your mom and you can hold the blessed feeling. The rest of the family can only imagine the feeling mom and son have together. It will always be a dear time in all our lives. Barbara and Ed's feelings are an important part. Nanna's (Ethyl) feelings with so many mixed emotions of the past and how life could have or should have been different!

Rita is so lucky to have a chance to share your life. Your children are beautiful in all ways. Your wife Barbara is one of the nicest ladies I've had a chance to meet.

I will not write too much about our family, for some day you can come to know us better. We've had our heartaches and crosses to bear.

We would like to thank you for the film and pictures. Absolutely beautiful, a story to be told and to hold. We would someday like to visit you.

We all will be thinking of you all.

Love,
Uncle George and Aunt Clara

The Mystery of Love

~ 9 ~

HIGH EXPECTATIONS

Not long after our fruitful visit, Rita contacted me and said she needed to share more details about her background and life. I, of course, agreed, and for the next hour or so, I sat motionless and wide-eyed.

"It was May 1946. I was eighteen. I was anxious to wear my new summer bathing suit. The suit was a daring white one-piece with shoulder straps, vertical color stripes, and an arresting design flair. I was Rita June Boomhower, and I wanted to be stunning. This was the day to test my new summer look at the pool. If I was right, someone intriguing might notice. My spirits were high, and the day was perfect for my debut.

"Almost a high school graduate I soon would accompany my parents to the Edgewood Falls Summer Resort they owned and managed. Our family resort was in East Durham, New York, a picturesque tourist hotspot in the Catskill Mountains, located about two hours north of New York City.

"I lived at on Newman Avenue in Bayonne, New Jersey with my mother, Ethyl May (Jennings), stepfather, Alex Stapchuk, (her second husband,) and my two siblings, brother George and sister Terry. My mother, Ethyl May Jennings, was born in Cairo, New York, in May 1903 and married her first husband, George Reed Boomhower. From this marriage, I was born along with my two brothers, George and Harold. Sadly, Harold, the oldest, later died in a shooting accident at age thirteen. My parents divorced not long after. Then, my fifty-five-year-old stepfather, Al Stapchuk, died in 1957. It was an unexpected shock. I adored my father."

"When my mother married her second husband, Alex J. Stapchuk, my half-sister, Terry, came into the world. Fourteen years younger than me, Terry instantly became an authentic "kid sister." My stepfather, Alex, legally adopted my brother, George, but I refused. I wanted to keep my birth father's name, Boomhower."

The pace quickened as Rita continued her story.

"My home was in Bayonne, a working-class neighborhood buzzing with young men just home from WWII and new immigrants trying to "move up the ladder." Some made it, others didn't.

"Reluctantly, I had ended my long relationship with my high school sweetheart, Tom Maloney. We started dating when I was fifteen. Although older, he was my first love. He enlisted in the Army when I was still in high school. Unfortunately, I learned during Tom's Army leaves, he had been unfaithful and cheated on me more than once. On military leave, instead of coming to see me, he 'played the field' and dated others. I think he made a fateful choice."

As Rita told her story it occurred to me that this woman was an original. She didn't try to be remarkable, she didn't put on airs, but she enjoyed being unforgettable. Not in a grand sweep of history way, but in the concentrated effort she put into everything she did. She was earnest, smart, and poised.

It was obvious that in the fashion world, Rita had control. If anyone was "dressed to the nines," Rita tried to be a ten. It didn't matter where she was going or what she was doing; she never left home without an air of cutting-edge fashion. Like a model, she understood how to pose long enough to display a shimmer of elegance. As a champion seamstress, she could add a swirl or a curl to any outfit and make it exquisite. In time, Rita fashioned her entire identity around her look and made it her own. In fashion, she had control. Now, her story began to sound like things in her life might spiral in a different direction.

Leaning forward, I heard the pitch of Rita's voice change as she explained what happened when she went to the pool in her new bathing suit.

"I sensed electricity in the air as I strolled across the pool deck. My suit was a hallmark look as I always tried to look better than everyone else. That day, I carried a conspicuous floral towel and fashion magazine and managed to snag a premium spot for my lounge chair. I could easily survey the crowd from my perch. Indifferently, I peered over the top of my magazine to see who was there with a fake air of indifference while harboring high expectations.

"On especially hot days, the whole neighborhood showed up. I hoped this was one of them. It was the place to be. Most of the faces were uninterestingly familiar until a young man popped up right in front of me. While still in the water up to his chest, he placed his tanned arms on the edge of the pool deck and introduced himself with a voice aching with hopefulness. "Hi, I'm Pat Ward. Haven't I seen you here before?"

"He had curly ringlets of ginger hair falling across his forehead. His face, handsome and angular, made me lose most of my well-disguised composure. I smiled and thought his opening introduction wasn't especially clever, but it would do. We began to talk.

"Patrick Ward, recently discharged from the Air Force, had flown with the Air Corps 8th Air Force in England as a B17 bombardier. He was twenty-four. I was mystified why I had never seen him, or maybe I just didn't remember. We traded the usual conversational questions as we became acquainted: Who do you know? Where'd you go to school? Where do you live? Pat described his hope of finding a job and using the GI Bill to further his education. He said his Irish family lived a few blocks away. He teased it would be easy for us to run into each other again."

Pat told Rita he lived with his parents, two brothers, (James) Jimmy and (John) Sean, and three sisters, Ann Marie, Susie, and Margaret. The Ward house was located in the shapeless shadow of low-income rental properties. Rita learned the Ward family sometimes moved a few blocks in the middle of the night to just avoid paying rent due on the first if they didn't have the money.

Mrs. Ward, as a centrifugal force, was a light-hearted woman. She had a most conspicuous maiden name: Grace Kelly. Everyone loved repeating her first and last name as a source of inspiration. She told everyone her namesake, Princess Grace of Monaco, once stated, "The idea of life as a fairy tale is a fairy tale."

In Ireland, Grace Kelly had married Pat's father in 1916 and had given birth to Susie and Margaret before arriving in America. Pat was born not long after they landed in Bayonne, New Jersey. Grace Kelly's special talent lay in her ability to nimbly switch her mood like running water from gravity to gaiety. She did her best to maintain household equilibrium by embracing an Irish thread: "Don't spread your cloak any farther than you can cover it."

Grace Kelly had the uncanny ability to establish a pattern of dignity and ceremony in almost everything. This talent helped the family endure and redeem their existence. Some days, it felt like the family was on a boat "shading off" as if shy of being seen with holy water tied to the prow. Household goings-on were filled with recitations from the dead and "doings" for the living, but fate always intervened. No matter how great the guarding was, sometimes simple bad luck snuck up on them when nobody saw it coming. There were times when they felt doomed and knew it.

Rita continued her story as I waited with all my questions:

"From the chance meeting at the Bayonne Pool, my affection for Pat bloomed. We shared mutual interests: swimming, dancing, telling jokes and stories, and having fun. Regularly, we went swimming, strolled for pizza, or grabbed a ten-cent movie and an ice cream. At Pat's house, we'd sometimes find his mother reading tea leaves for Sarah and James Bonner. Mrs. Bonner drank too much, and James, a destroyed war hero, frequently appeared lost. This compelled Grace Kelly Ward to be always kind with her advice. Staring at the tea leaves, she'd say, 'Ah, God loves you, Sarah. You've had a hard time, but I see everythin' improvin' for yourself, so ye be a little happier.'"

***

Pat's relationship with Rita became more serious when he invited her to his family's home for dinner. Naturally, Rita accepted. However, the invitation wasn't just about love but also self-preservation. Pat knew Rita's parents owned and managed a summer resort. He wanted to convince her to intercede on his behalf and help him get a job, and maybe his brothers, too. Inviting Rita to the Ward house was an act of hope, love, and desperation.

The Ward boys eagerly questioned Rita about her family's summer resort. They all wanted to know if Rita's family had any job openings, and if so, would she recommend them and ask her stepfather, Al, for an interview? Rita smiled and said, "Sure, I'll ask."

Arriving home, Rita quickly asked her mother if there were any job openings at the resort. "We're always looking for help and for anyone who will stay for the whole season."

The family's resort was a low-key establishment handed down to Rita's mother from her English parents, the Jennings. It offered modest, idyllic seasonal accommodations to a variety of vacationers, predominately English, Italians, and Irish from the surrounding New England states. The resort's advertisements touted the following:

"Come to the heart of the Catskill Mountains and enjoy a bountiful table supplied with fresh vegetables, chickens, eggs, and milk from our own farm. Within walking distance of Catholic churches and near other denominations. Swimming pool, cocktail lounge, outstanding cuisine, shuffleboard, air-conditioned motel, TV, and bicycling in the beautiful mountains where the air is clean, cool, and crisp. Clean, airy rooms with electric lights, showers, and baths for twenty dollars a week for two in a room. No guests

with contagious diseases accepted. You'll find your hosts, Al and Ethyl, keep an eye on things. They insist their resort does its best to please you...so you'll become one of those devoted and enthusiastic friends who return again and again. Make up a vacation party - Bring the family - We love people!"

Rita invited Pat and his brothers for lunch at their house as a pretext for a job interview. The three Wards boys put on their best clothes, smiled, and cranked up the blarney. They arrived at Rita's house, extended cordial greetings with a flourish, and made small talk with Rita's stepfather, Al Stapchuk.

Al announced, "I understand you boys are interested in summer job openings at our Edgewood Falls Resort?"

In unison, they echoed, "Yes."

With great fervor, the three young men regaled Al with all their prodigious skills and abilities, both real and imagined. They provided a constructive review of their experience, work ethic, and handiness. Al was especially pleased to hear about their wartime exploits. At the end, Al eyed the three boys and professed,

"Our summer resort offers lodging, food, and a reasonable wage with one day off on Sunday or Monday depending on your shift, but I only have openings for two of you."

The three boys eyed each other. Each hoped the other would volunteer to drop out of contention. Quickly, Pat decided he should take one of the jobs because he was the oldest. Sean would take the other job to help build physical strength in his injured leg from resort chores and fresh air. Jimmy announced he would work on the docks in Bayonne with his father. It was settled.

Within weeks, Rita and her Stapchuk family readied themselves for their seasonal move to Edgewood Falls. They had only a few weeks to prepare, new staff to train, a kitchen to stock, and cabins and rooms to be cleaned and readied. Although the season was short, generally coinciding with summer vacations, most of the Edgewood Falls clients were faithful regulars reserving dates for the year ahead when they departed. Families eagerly looked forward to their escape from urban life and the opportunity to see old friends. It sometimes felt like an annual family reunion.

~ 10 ~

A PLAN OF CONVENIENCE

It was June 1946, Rita's nineteenth birthday.

Her mother and father planned a special celebration: a surprise cake with candles for dessert while the resort guests sang "Happy Birthday." Rita loved the attention. She was flattered to receive all the birthday cards and greetings. After the celebration, some of the birthday crowd strolled to the resort's bar for after-dinner drinks. Although the drinking age was twenty-one, Rita had one or two celebratory birthday scotch and sodas disguised as ginger ale. It was a grand evening, and Rita was in high spirits. Pat and Rita were inseparable. They both were on stage and entertained the crowd with stories, songs, and jokes, then slipped away for some time together before the night was over.

***

Summer life at the resort developed its own rhythm. Pat, Rita, and Sean had daily chores, which was part of their commitment to keeping everything running smoothly. Rita was already adept at setting up and hosting guests in the dining room. Pat and Sean quickly became competent handymen, cleaning the pool, changing bedding arrangements in the cabins, and attending to multiple outdoor chores. There was always something to do throughout the day and evening. Free time found Rita and Pat lingering over a game, taking walks up to the waterfalls adjacent to the resort and otherwise satisfying young love.

One early August day, Rita was visibly distraught. She saw Pat and grabbed him by the arm. She asked to speak to him privately when he was free from work. Pat agreed. He said he would find her as soon as his shift was over. Pat began to wonder why Rita was so upset. It wasn't like her.

In a few short hours, they met alone. Pat gently asked, "Rita, what's the matter? Is something wrong? What's going on? You look like you've been crying."

Rita blurted, "My mother, Ethyl, had always told me,' to save myself,' but I never thought to ask, for what? Now, I know!" With tears welling in her eyes, she quietly whispered, "I think I'm a few months pregnant!"

Before Pat could respond, Rita plaintively asked, "What are we going to do?"

Pat choked, "Are you sure you're pregnant? How do you know?"

Rita said she had not been to a doctor yet, but all the symptoms were tell-tale. With tears streaming down her face, Rita implored, "What do you think we should do?"

Pat whispered, "I need to think about this. Does anyone else know you're pregnant?"

Rita blurted out, "God, no!!"

Pat mumbled, "Shh...not so loud; we need to keep this quiet. Don't tell anyone. Let's talk about this again tomorrow. I need some time to think about what to do. I'll come and find you when I have some answers."

Pat quickly ran to find his brother, Sean, to spill his guts about Rita's pregnancy. Sean told him that his brother and Rita had three choices: arrange an illegal abortion, keep the baby, or give it up for adoption.

The next morning, Pat said to Rita, "Your pregnancy is not what either of us expected, wanted, or even thought would happen. We were very naïve to not use any protection. I know getting married might seem like it would solve our problem, but it would be like putting a band-aid on an open wound. I don't think either of us is emotionally ready for marriage."

As Rita sputtered and cried, Pat quietly shared with her the three choices he and his brother Sean had discussed. First, Pat suggested arranging an abortion. If Rita could quickly find someone really good to perform an illegal procedure, it might be the best thing. It would certainly solve the problem. Next, he shared the other two options. Each suggestion started with the words, "You could." Pat's descriptions made Rita feel increasingly alone. The future looked bleak. The pregnancy was her problem. With welling emotion, she declared, "I'll see if I can get an abortion."

Tears rolled down Rita's cheeks. In her heart, she had guessed Pat's response. She knew he was right, but she wasn't prepared to hear the words spoken. Pat's true heart was revealed.

Rita knew the resort season was ending soon and that Pat and Sean would be leaving for their home in Bayonne. She now needed to find the right time to ask her parents for help. She longed for her mother's unswerving love and tenderness. Her mother always had an undefeatable ability to find acceptable and appropriate solutions to her daughter's mischievousness. This time, their secret would bond them together for a lifetime.

When the resort closed, the Stapchuk family was always the last to leave. They celebrated a good season only after the last task was completed and the property buttoned up for the winter. There was always much discussion about the season's highlights and prospects for the coming year. It was like color commentary during and after a football game. As usual, Al returned to temporary work in the Bayonne shipyards until spring.

In early October. Rita talked to her mother in the kitchen after her stepfather went to bed. She told her the whole story. She echoed everything Pat suggested and what she thought were her choices. Ethyl proposed a plan. First, she would have to share this news with Al, which would be a tough conversation. Second, she would arrange a discrete appointment with an out-of-town doctor to examine Rita and to see how far along she was. If Rita was still in her first trimester, then an abortion, although illegal, might be safe and relatively easy to arrange.

The next day, the family gathered. Al and Ethyl had come to an agreement. He muttered to Rita, "We all have to deal with your pregnancy. There are no other choices. You know your mother, and I love and support you. Do you want me to speak with Pat?"

Rita whispered, "I guess it would be okay, but I'm not sure it would do any good, since he's ready to leave soon to attend college in Colorado."

Pat had been clear about where he stood regarding her pregnancy, and she didn't want him to feel any pressure to marry her. This was devastating to Rita, but her foolish pride interfered with admonishing Pat for the decision he had made. She suggested that Al wait to speak with Pat until they have a better idea of options from the doctor. He reinforced Ethyl's plan to make an urgent doctor's appointment for Rita.

Several days later, a doctor examined Rita and then requested they meet in his office. Ethyl was hoping Rita's problem could soon be resolved. The awkward mess might finally be over if the doctor suggested he could fix everything. Everyone's life could return to normal.

The doctor said, "Rita, I am afraid you are pregnant and well past the first trimester. Your pregnancy is too far along for a safe abortion. I certainly wouldn't do it, and I don't believe any other respected physician would do so, either. It would be unwise to trust a physician willing to offer an abortion. Of course, the choice is up to you."

Arriving back at home, Ethyl took Rita aside and whispered, "Before we make final decisions, I want to try one idea we haven't considered. I will speak with your old boyfriend's mother, Mrs. Maloney. As you know, Tom was recently discharged from the military, and I've heard he's been asking about you."

Rita had dated and loved Tom during high school. They met when she was fifteen and were together for several years before he was drafted. Then, Tom had cheated on her. She looked at her mother and said, "If you want to speak with Mrs. Maloney, go ahead. I have nothing to lose."

When Ethyl spoke with Mrs. Maloney, she said, "As you may know, since Rita and Tom split-up she has dated other men, and we know Tom has dated other women. I was wondering if you thought Tom still had feelings for Rita?"

Mrs. Maloney replied, "I suppose, but isn't Rita seeing a neighborhood boy named Pat Ward? Didn't he work for you at the resort this past summer? Aren't they still dating? I imagined Pat and Rita's relationship must have blossomed?"

Ethyl said, "Yes, the relationship blossomed, but a little too far!"

In confidence, Ethyl then went on to explain the details of Rita's troubled situation. Mrs. Maloney took a deep breath. "How sad and unfortunate, but you know how these things happen. Please give Rita my love. What is she planning to do?"

Ethyl hedged, "I'm not sure, but an abortion is out of the question. I was thinking Tom might help."

Mrs. Maloney paused and wondered where Ethyl was going with that suggestion. She asked, "Help with what?"

Ethyl confessed, "If you think Tom still loves Rita, maybe the two of them might talk and consider getting married?"

Mrs. Maloney caught her breath, "I see, that's a lot to ask. May I call you in a day or two?"

A few days later, Mrs. Maloney called Ethyl. "Our son, Tom, says he still loves Rita and always has. He is willing to talk with her if she is willing. Maybe the two of them might mend some fences."

Rita called Tom, and they quickly agreed to meet that afternoon. They greeted each other with hugs and kisses, like old friends. After all, they had been sweethearts for a number of years. They walked and talked for an hour or more. It was clear whatever chemistry they once had still existed.

After a long talk, Tom said, "I think we should consider getting married. What do you think?"

"I would be happy to marry you, Tom, if you'll have me and my baby?"

"With a baby coming, we should probably get married soon before you begin to show too much. I don't want anyone to know you're pregnant. Let's leave it up to our parents to figure out what date might work best. The date doesn't matter to me as long as it's fast."

Tom said, "Well, if we're getting married, I have four non-negotiable requests. Actually, they're demands. I need to explain them to you, so you can decide if you still want to get married.

First, when we get married, we will immediately move from Bayonne to Vermont, where no one knows us. I have chosen the City of Rutland, where my family has a friend, Grace Lincoln. She has an empty apartment on Haskin's Avenue. We can live there while I look for a job, and you secretly have your baby.

"Second, after we settle in Rutland you will leave our apartment and travel two hours away to Burlington, Vermont to stay with the Sisters of Mercy. They manage the Bishop DeGoesbriand Hospital where you will have your baby and leave it there for adoption. The sisters have agreed to provide you lodging and meals as long as you pitch in to earn your keep."

"My third demand is most important. While you are at the hospital, you are to communicate with no one, not even your mother."

Tears streamed down Rita's face. Tom's demands were a continuing burden on her heart. She could already feel the baby move, and increasingly, she was more and more in love with the child she was carrying. How would she ever be able to give her child away?

"Finally, when you do return to me, your pregnancy will be our secret; only our parents will know, and no one else, ever!"

Rita thought a wedding with Tom would fix everything, but now she wasn't so sure. She needed to talk it over with her mother. Tom agreed Rita should weigh his marriage proposal in light of his demands. He knew she would be startled by his requests, even though he didn't feel his demands were unreasonable. He asked Rita to have a response by the next day as to whether the marriage would take place or not.

After talking to her mother, Ethyl took Rita's hand and looked at her directly, "Tom's conditions are tough, but they may be your best solution. This is all about what's best for you and for your baby. Unfortunately, you are not in a good bargaining position. Tom and his parents hold the cards. If you're willing, I think you should accept Tom's offer as it stands. Of course, the decision is yours, and I will support whatever you decide."

Rita answered with one word, "Yes."

~ 11 ~

CLOSED AND CONFIDENTIAL

On October 13, 1946, Rita June Boomhower married Tom Maloney.

After a brief honeymoon on Lake George, they settled into their new apartment in Rutland. Tom searched for a job. Some weeks later, Rita departed for her lengthy stay to have her baby at the Bishop DeGoesbriand Hospital in Burlington. Tom and Rita shared a warm kiss goodbye as she boarded the Greyhound bus.

Tom said, "I hope everything goes well. Remember to keep your promise not to share your secret with anyone. I'll see you in about four and a half months when you come back home."

Rita gave birth to a baby boy on March 26, 1947. At that time, babies scheduled for adoption did not have contact with their mothers. However, the nuns had grown fond of Rita during her stay with them and allowed her to choose a name. Rita chose Michael, after Saint Michael the Archangel, who she hoped would watch over her baby. On the official birth certificate and hospital records, Rita gave her husband's name, Tom Maloney, as the birth father.

As promised, a few days later, Rita returned to Tom in Rutland and started work at J. J. Newberry's, a local department store, where she was placed at the cosmetics counter. She never spoke again of her loneliness, her trauma, her baby, or her dreadful anguish, and Tom never asked.

***

As I listened to Rita's story, I easily recalled all of the same emotions and angst over the trauma of an unexpected pregnancy that I also experienced at the age of nineteen. Anxious to hear more, I reached for Rita's hand as she continued.

"I will only give you one bad example in our marriage. There are many more too unimaginable for you to know. I never knew where Tom was. He came home most nights from the local bar at two a.m. Upon arrival, he'd place a loaded pistol on the kitchen table and demand some dinner. Then, when I reheated and fixed his dinner, he'd pull the tablecloth and send everything crashing to the floor, demanding I prepare him a fresh meal. One night, he even played Russian roulette with me. I was terrified every day. My life with Tom was a nightmare. We divorced on October 4, 1955, based on 'intolerable severity and persistent refusal or neglect to support.'"

After hearing Rita's story and talking to others, I was able to piece together more of the puzzle to understand what had happened to me. Apparently, I remained in the hospital nursery for a month, waiting for a bed at Saint Joseph's Orphanage and Asylum, managed by the Sisters of Providence from Montreal, Canada. In the early years after WW II, many orphanage children were not actually orphans but were frequently left for periods of time until parents could get "back on their feet." Like me, most orphanage children came from families in the region.

All adoptions until late in the twentieth century were closed and confidential. This was perceived as a way to enable parents and children to avoid the family stigma of illegitimacy. Records were sealed to all but the people directly involved. Even the names of witnesses to an adoption were refused access. The Catholic Charities were strict agencies following church traditions of a family – man and woman – and offered adoptive parents a chance to raise a child without fear of intrusion by biological parents.

The orphanage children were left by single or divorced mothers and even married adults who were ill, addicted, jailed, or down on their luck. Some were extremely poor or, in some circumstances, violent. However, most believed they were delivering their child to a safe place.

Frequently, children didn't fully grasp they were being abandoned at the orphanage until the moment they turned around and discovered whoever delivered them was gone. The Office of Catholic Charities represented the orphanage as the official adoption agency. All adoptions were a solemn affair. Considerable effort was made to ensure an optimal match of ethnicity between the adoptive parents and the child, which made foster parenting a criterion for adoption.

In 2018, Vermont's *Seven Days* newspaper described the St. Joseph's Orphanage and Asylum as an "imposing structure situated on a rise of land on the eastern shore of Lake Champlain and next to an adjacent cemetery in Burlington, Vermont. The institution was neither a jolly nor pleasant place to be. In fact, it was not an especially safe place, especially for helpless babies. St. Joseph's was its own little universe, sometimes governed by a cruel logic, hidden behind brick walls."

Behind the orphanage's heavy doors was an expansive interior. It had three floors, a cavernous attic with twelve-foot-high ceilings and enormous windows. The attic space was a shadowy chamber, which covered the length and breadth of the building. It was eerie and disorienting, scattered with draped religious statues and large stored church artifacts. Most days orphans traveled to the attic, two at a time, to retrieve clothes from a cubby or hanging on a hook, and warm jackets for outdoor playtime.

The corridors were long with dorm rooms right and left containing multiple beds sorted by age. The walls were plaster over brick with scuffed-up wainscoting to protect the surface from children. It was austere, mostly functional, and sparse.

Later investigations reported: "Older orphans were frequent babysitters. Some claimed the nuns did cruel things to helpless babies. One orphan claimed she saw a nun hold a baby's head underwater to stop it from crying. Another said if babies continued to whine, some nuns would cover their mouths until they turned blue. Infants were known to die of meningitis, malnutrition, and dehydration."

The level of neglect strained credulity, but it happened. "The Sisters of Providence explained to every orphan babysitter that the little babies were 'bad' boys and girls from 'bad' mothers. The babies were 'little bastards' and therefore didn't deserve affection and coddling."

Investigations suggested even some priests and lay people employed by the orphanage abused those they were charged to keep safe. "Older orphans were warned 'don't tell anyone' about what they heard or witnessed at St. Josephs. If they did, they would never be adopted or see their parents again. With the doors of St. Joseph's shut behind them, the orphans played a strange pivotal role in a private theatre, with many actors but no audience."

Names were not given to orphaned babies. Children were assigned an identity number, and the nuns addressed each orphan by their number, not a name. Clothes were hung from numbered pegs in closets matching the child's identification number. Children were lined up and proceeded to retrieve their clothes for the day. The nuns would call out, "Numbers twenty-three and thirty-seven, you're next.

Essentially, the orphanage seemed like a pit of despair, a place where the staff did not always look out for the welfare and safety of the children who were abandoned there and waiting for someone to rescue them.

I was lucky. Someone did!

Prying Open the Last Secret

~ 12 ~

THE EXTRA SON

Dear Mr. Ward,

I am writing to you with a story you may find quite interesting. This letter is a beginning.

I was born in Burlington, Vermont, on March 26, 1947, and a month later placed at the St. Joseph's Orphanage and Asylum for adoption with Vermont Catholic Charities. I have attached some of the earlier correspondence with them. After several months, I was taken by William and Mary Luck as a foster child and possible adoption. Two years later, the Lucks legally adopted me.

I had a wonderful life attending Catholic Schools in an Irish Democratic family.

In 1993, my adoptive mother died in Florida, and I still care for my eighty-seven-year-old adoptive father. The death of my mother and my aging father made me finally realize it was getting late if I had any interest in finding my biological parents. This interest was particularly heightened because I have three children and a grandson with nothing to tell them about their ancestral or genetic past. Having spent ten years in healthcare administration, I've been acutely aware one's future (health) depends a great deal on one's genetic legacy. With the possibility of more grandchildren on the way, I felt any information would be nice.

I utilized an adoption search consultant located in St. Albans, Vermont. In a short time, my birth mother, Rita, was located in Rutland, Vermont. We met for an emotional reunion several years ago. I was the only child she ever had. During the past four years, we have visited often, talked by telephone, and, as a family, taken trips to Spain and Italy. She attended my oldest son's wedding (Sean Michael), my only daughter's (Holly Marie) college graduation, and several of our youngest son, Jonathan Wilson Luck's, piano recitals. He is in high school.

Rita kept you a secret from me by suggesting her first husband, Tom Maloney, long deceased, was my father. However, after several years, she decided to tell the truth. When I asked her about my birth father, she pulled out an old black & white photo, hidden for a half-century, of you two by a swimming pool. She pointed and said, "This is me, and the man with his arm wrapped around me is your father, Patrick J. Ward."

My birth mother is Rita June Boomhower/Stapchuk. She divorced Tom Maloney when she was twenty-seven and remained single for many years until she remarried Edward Mills, Jr. at the age of forty-five.

You recall when you and Rita parted, she was pregnant. Unfortunately, arranging an abortion was impossible. She married her old boyfriend Tom Maloney and, through friends, moved to Rutland, Vermont, to keep the pregnancy a secret. Tom Maloney insisted Rita give me up for adoption and never tell anyone. She gave birth to me at nineteen years of age, and for reasons even she can't quite explain (mostly pride), she couldn't or wouldn't tell you the truth.

Rita stayed with the Sisters of Mercy at the Bishop DeGoesbriand Hospital in Burlington, Vermont, gave birth, and went back to her husband. Only Rita's and Tom Maloney's parents know what she did. Rita's brother, George, and sister, Terry, had no idea. Rita never even told her current husband, Eddie. As you might guess, he was not happy when he found out. Rita's mother, Ethyl Stapchuk, now resides in a nursing home in the Catskills.

This whole story is not your fault. Well, some of it is. Rita never told you the truth. Naturally, because she was unable to obtain an abortion. I got a lucky break.

I enclose some photos from the past, including the one with you and Rita by the pool. Other photos are of my family. In order to be totally transparent, I have also enclosed my academic résumé so you can see I've had a wonderful life and professional career, so I am not suddenly looking for anything other than an opportunity to communicate with you. I do not wish to intrude on your life.

It would be nice to have a few photos of your family as well as aunts and uncles. It would be thrilling if you might even consider coming to Boston to see your grandchildren and great-grandson, Patrick Ryan Luck, who was born on February 24.

I know this letter is undoubtedly mindboggling for you and most likely an emotional overload. Imagine what it is for me to be writing this letter. I wonder what you must be thinking and feeling. I will gladly accept and understand if your family situation makes all my hopefulness impossible. On the other hand, if we both have a chance to get to know one another, that would be most enjoyable.

Please call, write, fax, or e-mail.
I look forward to hearing from you.
With warm regards,
Michael Luck

I mailed my letter and waited, and waited, and waited.

***

Finally, Pat apparently decided to put the paternity question to rest, and he wrote a response six weeks later.

July 1997
Dear Michael,
The news in your letter was certainly a shocking surprise. For a number of reasons, I may not be your biological father. However, if you wish, you can remove any ambiguity by doing a DNA test, with which I shall cooperate. Your life has been indeed a great success with a wonderful family and the wonderful accomplishments both academic and in your professional life.

Considering genetic traits, both my family history and I are blessed with a complete lack of any genetic defects, and we all continue to enjoy considerable longevity. Presently, I am seventy-five years old and in good physical condition without any aches and pains.

I am pleased you are enjoying an ongoing activity with your birth mother and had such loving and caring parents during your life. However, I feel at the present time, it would be most traumatic to both our families should anything be disclosed to them and would serve no purpose.

Sincerely,

Pat

I discovered later that much internal machination took place before he was able to respond. Pat said that he had read my handwritten letter over and over. He didn't know the man writing the letter, but he knew Rita. The letter's contents left him stunned. He admitted that he was flabbergasted. The dates, names, and facts were all familiar. Yes, it was him in the poolside photo. The information was half-century old, and it was almost all true, except for one glaring detail. I had claimed to be his child. This was surely a mistake.

He knew Rita had been pregnant but was certain she had an abortion. That's what they had agreed to do, and he had heard nothing different. She had never suggested any other course of action. When Pat left Rita at the resort at the end of the season, neither one communicated with the other. The big clincher for Pat was that he actually saw Rita one and half years later after they parted when he traveled to New Jersey for a holiday break from college. He spoke with her for the first time when he invited Rita to see him in New York, and she agreed. When they met, she never said anything about a baby. Then again, he remembered, he never asked her either.

Pat shared my letter with his wife, Donna. She read it carefully. If the letter were true, it would throw a "monkey wrench" into their family dynamics and relationship with their four sons and everyone else. The truth now was that Pat's oldest son was possibly the man writing the letter. This concept of a new, unknown family member would be difficult to assimilate into their lives.

Donna read the letter twice. She memorized each detail. She asked, "Pat, is this true? I remember you talked about the Stapchuks and the resort where you and Sean worked when we first met. You didn't mention you had a relationship with the boss's daughter, got her pregnant, and then never knew she had your child? Are you the father? Why is this man, Michael, so sure it's you? If you're not, we need to confirm you're not his father, so he can search elsewhere... unless you are his father and we now have a bigger family."

Pat said, "I don't know. I'm unsure if the letter is entirely true. The man who wrote this letter can't be my son. He just can't be. Yes, I got Rita pregnant, but she had an abortion. It was so long ago. I have to think about this for a while before I respond."

Donna declared, "Pat, this is important. A long-lost child is not something easily dismissed. We have some work to do."

Pat tried to recall all the details about dating Rita and the dreadful moments of discussing what should be done about her pregnancy. He dredged up memories long forgotten and tried to understand what was real and what might have been wishful thinking. If he wrote to me, he had to decide what he would reveal and what he would withhold. This was a matter of self-protection and pride. He knew Rita had planned an abortion, or it's what he understood. He had heard nothing to the contrary. If the man writing this letter existed, it sure would be a surprise to have a fifth son at seventy-five years of age! He already had four sons who he adored.

Weeks passed. Pat poured over my letter again and again, hoping to find a fatal flaw, something he could pick apart to derail my supposition. How could he have an extra son? In a moment of doubt, Pat shared the letter with his son, Rich, and wife, Ellen, who were visiting from their overseas home in Leiden, Netherlands. Pat handed Rich the letter and said, "Hey, check this out and tell me what you think."

Rich read the letter and then reread it. There was a long silence as if he wasn't sure what to say. The letter appeared to be a thorough and concise account of a portion of his father's early life before he met and married his mother, Donna.

Rich asked, "Is this true, Dad? Do we have another brother?"

This was not exactly the response Pat was expecting. With a dramatic wave of his hands, Pat pronounced, "How the hell do I know? I dated Rita for a period of time. Your Uncle Sean and I worked at her family's resort one summer, but it's news to me if she had my baby. If she did, I'm virtually certain it's not mine." Of course, Pat had to know he wasn't telling the whole truth. He knew Rita was pregnant and assumed Rita had taken care of the problem before he moved to Colorado. Pat added, "I even saw Rita in New York City more than a year and a half after we broke up, and she never said anything about a baby."

Despite his doubts, it was thrilling to receive Pat's letter, however brief. I thought I might never receive a response. Although the tone of the letter was a bit distant, unsure, and reserved, that was understandable. Pat suggested a paternity test would solve the ambiguity. This was a huge step toward resolution, and I appreciated his willingness to cooperate.

Quickly, I responded,

July 31, 1997
Dear Mr. Ward,
Thank you for responding to my earlier letter to you. I suspected my correspondence would be a shock for you and might cause great concern. There was no easy way for me to introduce the probability I may be your son. I understand your reservations and appreciate your reluctance to communicate with me in any detailed manner until you have more valid evidence that we have an irrefutable genetic connection.

Upon your advice, I have contacted the Boston Blood Center next to Brigham's and Women's Hospital. The center conducts all DNA testing in the region. I am asking if you might go to Alta Bates Hospital, near your home in Berkeley, on the morning of August 11. Register on the first floor admitting station for outpatients. A blood testing kit from the Boston Blood Center will be waiting for you. I already paid for the test. Our (you, me, and Rita) blood samples will be sent by Federal Express back to the center, and they will report the results to all three of us.

Thank you, once again, for your reply to my letter and especially your willingness to participate in a blood test to erase any doubts. It is my hope that we will have an opportunity to communicate at greater length in the future.

P.S. I enclose a few photos taken a few weeks ago of the old Catskill resort in New York. After the fire and rebuilding I am sure it looks different from the old days. My wife, Barbara, and I went with Rita to see Ethyl Stapchuk (my grandmother) in a nursing home. Sadly, she continues to decline since we first saw her. She is now completely blind.

Ethyl wanted me to apologize to you for giving you the cold shoulder when you stopped by to visit her and Uncle George several years ago. She knows your visit was meant to be a trip down memory lane. But she knew you did not know Rita had your baby and gave it up for adoption. Her cold shoulder was because she hadn't quite forgiven you for leaving Rita in a lurch. She's sorry. She realizes the way she acted was wrong.

By the way, Pat, Rita's mother, sent her a Mother's Day card every year for a half-century. Rita's second husband, Eddie, who didn't know she had delivered a baby, thought his mother-in-law was a little daft.

Warm regards,
Michael

We made arrangements for three blood tests. Pat, Rita, and I went to separate healthcare facilities to have blood drawn and test material returned to the Boston DNA Center. Within a week, an official envelope arrived in the mail. It was the moment of truth. I felt like a prospective college-bound student receiving a letter of decline or acceptance, except the stakes were so much higher. I slowly opened the envelope as if careful reverence might skew the outcome.

The letter was addressed to Pat Ward dated September 19, 1997. The letter was copied to both Rita and to me.

It stated:

Dear Mr. Ward,

Michael Luck has asked me to communicate to you the results of the recent blood tests done at CBR Laboratories. A complete copy of the results is enclosed.

The conclusion of the test results indicates there is a 99.78% chance of paternity when comparing your blood sample against Michael Luck's. In other words, the likelihood you are his biological father is extremely likely; 99.83% of falsely accused men would be excluded as the father in the above test.

Enclosed are details affirming the DNA test.

Sincerely,
Mary Barker, M.D.
Harvard Community Health Plan
David H. Bing, Ph.D.
Director of the CBR Clinical Testing Laboratory

I was thrilled and wondered how Pat might feel when reading the results. Now, the search was over, and the mystery had been solved. Pat Ward was my biological father. I let that sink in for a moment.

Anticipating an emotional phone call or letter from Pat, I waited for days. No call came; instead, there was silence and no letter or communication of any kind. I considered writing to Pat but decided to be patient. The ball was properly in his court. He was the one who wanted to be sure of his paternity, and now he was.

More than a month went by.

I finally got impatient and wrote on October 28, 1997.

Dear Pat,
Greetings!!

Fall in New England has been spectacular this year, and during my walks with my wife, Barbara, I find myself thinking of you. We wonder if you enjoy this time of year in Berkeley as much as we do. I hope so.

I have not heard from you since the DNA test results confirmed I am your biological son. I am left to presume you are experiencing a full range of feelings, just as Rita did a few years ago when I found her. I hope you will be receptive to my sharing with you some of my own feelings. It is a chance to communicate with you at a time when you may be sorting through similar emotions.

First, I want to thank you for suggesting the DNA test as a way to erase the ambiguity of paternity. Now the story is indisputable. For me, there is a sense of relief and pride knowing who represents my natural heritage. I am glad to know it is you, especially because Rita speaks so warmly of you, your parents and siblings.

As you know from my previous correspondence, I was given an Irish Catholic identity by my adoptive parents, Bill and Mary Luck. My identity has been comfortable and strong. Naturally, when I learned of Rita's German/English heritage, I was challenged to view myself somewhat differently. Certainly, knowing you are a first-generation Irish whose father, Patrick, and mother, Grace Kelly, were born in Ireland intrigues me and validates my adoptive identity.

Rita has spoken often about you and your family. She fondly remembers Jimmy and Sean, as well as your sisters. She vividly recalls the summer you and Sean were at her family's summer resort. Naturally, she adored each moment of her time with you. It was her first time experiencing love.

I am curious how you ended up in Berkeley and whether your sisters, Anne Marie, Margret, and Susie, settled in New Jersey or elsewhere. Since I have often moved with my work in hospitals and universities I wonder if this nomad existence and adaptability is a Ward family trait.

As a man, I take pride in my work and believe I have made and continue to make a satisfactory contribution to my profession. Again, Rita tells me she thought you spent time in the Middle East (Tehran?) working in the oil business. Given that my oldest son, Sean, graduated from Worcester Polytechnic Institute with a major in computer science and electrical engineering, I wonder if his scientific mind comes from your side of the family. This is especially curious because my other son, Jonathan (fifteen years of age), also loves computers, mathematics, and music.

Rita shared with me her memory of your family being musically and theatrically inclined. I love theatre. It has been a curiosity of mine that we all seem to play ourselves as a part. Indeed, I sometimes plan events with a theatrical flair. I sang in choirs and a folk singing group when I was young, and I have always loved theatre. Once, I won the Vermont One Act Play competition in high school. Moreover, we are a family with a quick wit and a great sense of humor. I can only imagine many of these traits may come from your side of the family.

As you know, I am sensitive to the fracture in my family (my divorce twenty years ago from the mother of my two oldest children). The divorce was complicated by my work around the country, which created an unfortunate distance from my children. I think this made us all value family much more. Yes, the children and I have experienced hardship due to the choices made. However, we have also learned the hard lessons that come from the hurt endured through separation. What we have is a deeper sense of tolerance for the complex composition of family. First, as a nuclear one, and then with step-grandparents, stepmothers, and step-aunts and uncles. With both biological birth parents, I have new family members to know and cherish.

With adult children, my family understands difficult choices are made with varying outcomes. As a family, we are fortunate our children learn to accept us recognizing our strengths and weaknesses. Rita learned the hurt and pain endured from choices she made from what she describes as "foolish pride."

Rita's brother, George, and sister, Terry, were thrilled to learn Rita had a child. It was a secret until recently. Rita never told them, so they never knew. Rita is now free to let go of some of her past, which has haunted her. At seventy years of age, she can be liberated by the truth.

When I go for walks, I try to think of ways I might build trust with you. I wonder why at seventy-six years of age you are worried about what your family might think about something which was an accident fifty years ago.

I wonder why you seem uncomfortable communicating with someone who is as much your son (at least genetically) as any other child you have. The volume of Ward blood is exactly the same.

My wife, Barbara Wilson, is supportive. She understands my longing and curiosity in knowing you exist, but not knowing if I will ever be given the opportunity to know you. With a grandchild I am acutely aware of the brief time we have in life. During your remaining years, I hope I can learn more about you and pass that along, with pride, to my children and grandchildren.

I hope you will write and cultivate some connection.
Let's not lose the opportunity to get to know one another.
With warm regards,
Your son,
Michael

~ 13 ~

FOR THOSE LIVING ALONE

Rita insisted that she write to Pat to explain why she kept my birth a secret from him and everyone else. She felt like Pat was blaming everyone except himself for his surprising news. With her deep sense of remorse, Rita was compelled, once again, to clear the air and her conscience.

October 1997
Dear Pat,
How little do we realize our decisions end up affecting so many others? I caused a lot of pain to others and endured a lot of heartache. With maturity, you learn that "sorry" is a poor and inadequate word. You are powerless to undo what you did.
When I realized I was pregnant, my mother and father took me to the doctor. He said the pregnancy could not be terminated. I decided not to tell anyone about what had happened. Pride is hell. I felt I had to get over you. So, I called you on the telephone to confirm I was getting an abortion. I only told my mother and father as well as my old boyfriend, Tom Maloney, so he would support an engagement to be married. Tom was wild about my pregnancy. He insisted I had to go away and have my baby with the nuns at a Catholic hospital and then come home. I did this all alone. I've gone through a great deal with family, friends, and my second husband, Edward, since Michael found me.

After giving Michael away, Tom would not have children for his own reasons. Contrary to your thoughts, I never had sexual relations with him before you. This fact didn't help when I was pregnant from you. Tom and I had been together off and on since age fifteen, but he cheated on me while he was in the military service around the time I met you. As you so well know, you awakened an emotional tidal wave I wasn't prepared to deal with. I wasn't able to control it.

I want you to know you're giving me our son was a most precious gift, even if it took so long for him to find me. I now realize how deeply I felt the loss. You go on with your life, but you're not whole. Now, I have grandchildren and a great-grandchild as well as my son.

I have told him many wonderful stories about you and your family. Although I can never get back the years lost, I'm determined with the time I have left to make up for all the love I missed. I am trying to undo all the hurt. Michael's family is so wonderful to me.

Meeting you, his father is his dream. No way do we know what's around the corner in our lives. I know I didn't. After Michael discovered me, I cried almost every day for a year. Then, the shock of it hit me and I realize above all else, God has given me this moment in my life and I am most grateful. I hope you are also blessed with children and grandchildren and have a good life. Michael is my miracle. Forgive me.

Rita

Rita told me that she hoped her letter to Pat might help encourage a closer connection. Several weeks went by and a letter from Pat finally arrived. I slowly opened it.

November 11, 1997

Dear Michael,

You are right — on receiving the shocking news from the lab. I was undecided how to handle the situation. Suffice it to say, it was a miracle you were born and then had a wonderful nurturing life with caring parents who raised you as their own son and enabled you to become educated at the highest level. Regardless of biology, it is they who should be considered as your real mother and father.

I have not and do not intend to tell my family of my connection with you. It would be much too disruptive for a variety of reasons and only create negative results. My feeling is a child and man develop attitudes, judgment, and values from the example and guidance of the parents who raise them regardless of biological birth. Obviously, you have been most fortunate. I share your feeling the Luck family gave you the opportunity to have a fruitful happy life. It is something we can all be most grateful for, as you turned out so well with a wonderful family.

You did, however, express an interest in me sharing information with you concerning my background and current status. I shall be glad to share with you a brief sketch of my life. As surmised, I am presently 75 years old and, fortunately, in excellent health, an avid golfer with a keen interest in sports. During WWII, I was in the Air Corps 8th Air Force in England, dropping bombs in Germany. After my time with Rita, I went to Colorado to go to college on the GI Bill. Later, I spent almost half of my life working overseas.

A summary follows:

1950 BA Economics (cum laude) University of Colorado

1950-1951 Graduate Study for a Ph.D. (Discontinued to accept a job.)

1951-1953 Labor Economist-U.S. Department of Labor

1953-1962 Arabian American Oil Company-Dhahran, Saudi Arabia, Senior Research Manager

1962-1970 Oil Consortium, Tehran, Iran - Exxon Loan Employee Economics and Management Manager

1970-1979 Bechtel Corporation - San Francisco, CA
International Manpower Services Manager

1979-1986 Consulting to Oil Companies in the Arabian Gulf - Athens, Greece

1986-1994 Private consulting overseas on an ad hoc basis

1994 - Return to golf, traveling, and other interests

We celebrated our 50th Anniversary of marriage in 2000, with all four sons born overseas in Dhahran and raised in Iran. The youngest is the only one following an engineering career in hydrology and environmental areas. The others are either writers or associated with creative work. All have advanced degrees. They each decided not to attend a university their brothers attended, so their selections varied.

#1 son Harvard undergrad and then Law School
#2 son UC Berkeley undergrad and then an MBA
University of Geneva, Switzerland
#3 son Cornell University undergrad and then an MFA
#4 son Stanford University undergrad and then M.S.
Geology and Earth Sciences

All are happily married. We have eight grandchildren. My sisters, Susan and Margaret, died long ago. Jim, John (Sean), and Ann Marie are still hale and hearty, and we see one another as often as possible. My major avocation is sports and theatrical productions. I have acted and directed a large number of plays. After Tehran, where my boys went to a mission school, we returned to the U.S. and Berkeley in 1970. We left for Athens in 1979 when the boys were out of high school, maintaining our home in Berkeley while away.

Give my regards to Rita. Tell her under the circumstances she did the noble and right thing to have you happily raised by the wonderful Luck family.

With fond regards,
Pat Ward

Pat's letter was both intriguing and somewhat disappointing. He was obviously reluctant to weave me into his life, which was understandable. Pat wanted the secret to continue.

I had always suspected Pat was betting the DNA test to exonerate him. He'd be off the hook, and I could continue my search for my biological father elsewhere. Pat's letter didn't seem to suggest that the surprise of his fatherhood had brought any particular fondness or pleasure. It seemed he was still in a state of shock but diplomatic. Pat had taken great pains to appropriately give credit to my adoptive parents, even though his comments seemed a bit deflective.

Of course, I loved my adoptive parents more than anything in the world, but it didn't mean there wasn't room for another loving relationship. At least, I thought Pat's letter was warmer than the previous correspondence. He had signed it in a friendly manner, "With fond regards," which may be what surprised fathers say.

I felt a bit silly putting so much emphasis on the closing of a letter, but I was desperate for any clues about this man. Those few words that end a letter can shed so much light on the sender's state of mind. I, of course, wanted it to be quite personal and familiar, an indication of how he was feeling without being demonstrative. After all, here was a man who was raised when emotions were not encouraged, particularly within the same gender. So, was his curt, somewhat professional sendoff simply a result of his upbringing, or was he signaling for me to keep my distance? One thing was crystal clear: it created more questions than answers.

When I next spoke with Rita, I read Pat's correspondence. All of her feelings and fears resurfaced. She was happy a connection with Pat had been made, and despite his reticence to share my existence with his family, she still thought things might work out in time. I did not immediately reply to Pat's 1997 letter while wrestling with how I should address my response to Pat: "Dear Mr. Ward, Dear Dad, Dear Father, or Dear Pat." The salutation was important. I didn't want Pat to feel I was overstepping boundaries and moving too fast, so I chose to remain respectful and formal.

March 5, 1998

Dear Mr. Ward,

Thank you for your letter of November 12th. My tardiness in replying to your kind letter is due to a number of factors.

First, I felt some time to process all the news and let it settle was important for both of us.

Second, the demands of my frantic professional and family life, combined with teaching a new University course in the evening, have been overwhelming.

> *I hope your birthday, along with holiday celebrations, was the most enjoyable. We enjoyed Thanksgiving with our son, Sean, and his wife, Gail, and our first grandson, Patrick Ryan Luck. No, my son did not know about you when he named our grandson. Further, I took the name "Patrick" as my Catholic confirmation name over thirty-six years ago. Perhaps it is just an interesting coincidence.*
>
> *I was delighted to receive your letter and to be introduced to a sketch of your life and your four sons. I found it interesting your sons accomplished their education at some of the finest and most prestigious institutions of higher learning. You must be proud of them. I hope their careers are as satisfying to them as mine has been for me.*

I then went on to describe my academic study, recent travel with Barbara and Jonathan to London, and a planned trip to China after a sixteen-year absence. I tried to include anything I thought might capture his attention and interest, including a recent conference in Texas where I made a presentation on the "Anthropology of American Humor." It was similar to the course I previously taught at Rutgers University in the evening after work. Near the end of the letter to Pat, I tackled the concept of "nurture versus nature."

> *While I agree wholeheartedly that my adoptive parents are "my parents" – and I love them dearly and always will — one cannot escape the perennial academic argument of "nature vs. nurture." My view is "the fruit doesn't fall far from the tree." No matter how much and how different the nurturing or raising of a child might be, the genes control or lend strength to a person's destiny, intellect, interests, musical talents, language skills, as well as physical attributes, health, and longevity. My search for your whereabouts was not to find a "father." I already have one. Instead, my search was to connect with my genetic legacy. Just like your sons, I, too, am endowed with the exact number of Ward genes. Yes, some distinction comes from having different mothers, but nonetheless, it is a heritage mutually shared. Recently, when our son Jonathan was voted to an All-Star cast in Winter Week plays, we celebrated his talents with thoughts of you. It is*

one of the joys of parenthood to know the excitement of sharing inherited talents with one's child.

I respect your wishes not to tell your family about me. Even so, I must confess to a feeling of excitement at the prospect of growing to know your four sons, with whom I imagine I share many similar interests. Having the experience of getting to know and laugh with them would be a great pleasure. Of course, I am interested in knowing you, too. However, I recognize that my existence might be more challenging to integrate. Discomfort is understandable. On the other hand, your sons may not have these same barriers to overcome.

Given I was created over a half-century ago, long before you met your wife, I should be non-threatening. So, you have five sons, one of whose existence was kept from you for over fifty years! It's a big deal and not so big at the same time. No one wants anything from you or your family other than, perhaps, time and intellect. As I have shared with you in previous letters, you did nothing wrong. No apologies need to be made to anyone. You were never given the opportunity to respond until now. Among men, I believe the potential for an unknown child is always possible.

In the time we have, I am happy to write to you. Even in the routine moments there are some things to be shared, a connection to be made. Usually, once a year, I get to California on university business. As the year unfolds, perhaps we could plan a meeting, or a lunch somewhere at your convenience? It would be wonderful to see you. Write again soon whenever you can. I would love to hear from you.

Warm regards,
Michael

It was clear that Pat did not want to talk by telephone; maybe it was too intimate and personal, and he didn't want to get that close. Unfortunately, my lethargy at writing letters was episodic, but Pat's communication was even more intermittent. My experience getting to know Rita was almost totally the opposite of my interaction with Pat. Rita had taught me patience was required. Pat's insistence that only he and his wife Donna should know of my existence might be a disappointment only for the moment.

I did not push the idea of growing closer to Pat out of proper protocol. In three years of writing to each other, there was never a telephone call, but the letters continued, and they were increasingly informative.

Each year, Pat sent me his annual Ward Family Christmas Newsletter. Each one began with tantalizing insight and humorous anecdotes, such as the story of his granddaughter, Kyra. Apparently, Pat had taken a magic course so he could entertain his grandchildren on Thanksgiving. He intended to perform his new-found dazzling illusion skills to entertain family members. On Thanksgiving Day, with more than a dozen family members convened, was the moment for Pat's well-rehearsed mystifying cup and ball trick involving dexterity and clever sleight of hand.

Granddaughter Kyra stood on a chair, scrutinizing her magical grandfather with an eagle eye. Soon, Pat's well-earned applause turned to riotous laughter as Kyra, with uncanny or purposefully poor timing (or both?), spread her arms as Pat completed his trick and prematurely exclaimed, "Ta-Da." The audience was convulsed by Kyra's innocent destruction of her grandfather's magic show. In response, the itinerant veteran showman switched gears to unveil his "mind-reading" performance. Kyra, apparently not a granddaughter to be easily dismissed from center stage, began to inject nonsense words and non-sequiturs to disrupt the mind-reading trick. Joyful tears flowed from Pat's audience as raucous laughter brought the show to an ignominious close. Pat crumpled up his props, thoroughly defeated by a three-year-old scene stealer of major talent. He announced magic shows should only be performed if kids are locked up or booked for their own comedy routine downtown. Secretly, Pat rejoiced in his granddaughter's command of the stage. She was a "chip off the old block."

Quickly, I dashed off a note.

February 22, 1999
Dear Mr. Ward,
We all laughed at the story of Patrick Ward, The Wizard of Magic, trying to compete with his granddaughter for attention. How brave and foolish you were. We, too, find grandchildren to be formidable competition. In many ways, they are not really competition. They always win! Regardless of the outcome, the truth is you and Kyra created a memorable moment for your family. In reality, it was all you were shooting for. Well done!

One Ward Family Christmas letter was a revelatory nugget of gold. Although I had already done some sleuthing about where each of my half-brothers went to college, I now knew they had recently made a presentation together at the National Arts Club (NAC) in New York. The presentation was a spirited slide show about the family's trip to Iran in search of their beloved caretaker and houseman, Hassan, and his family from years past when they lived there. All of Pat's boys had grown up with Hassan as a guide, teacher, and ever-present source of inspiration while their father worked for an oil company.

I called the National Arts Club inquiring about how to purchase a copy of a recording or video of the Ward brothers' presentation, "Searching for Hassan." The National Arts Club sent back a VHS tape in a padded envelope. Now, I had a front-row seat to see my four brothers in action for the first time, as well as a glimpse into their personalities, styles, and humor. I watched the video over and over, mesmerized by their manner and substance. The style, gestures, and voice inflections were familiar; they were mine, too. I learned of their spirited, good nature and hilarious behavior during their youthful years growing up in Iran, as well as their more recent arduous travel to recapture the past.

Kevin, the oldest brother, with a distinct flair for mixing subtle humor with practical details, led the video presentation. He remarked that "Searching for Hassan" was about seven headstrong travelers (Pat, Donna, and his three brothers, with a driver and government guide). The family needed a leader and only achieved anarchy. Kevin's brother, Terry, eventually published an internationally bestselling book about their travels entitled, "Searching for Hassan," which described the five decision-making rules the family assiduously followed.

They were:

1. Someone makes a suggestion.
2. Then, each person makes fun of the suggestion.
3. Then, everyone makes fun of the person who made the suggestion.
4. Then, someone comes up with a different insane idea because it is the opposite of the first suggestion.
5. And then, finally, the winner is the person who manages to remain focused long enough to keep yelling.

The video was a treasure. I never told Pat I had seen it. Now, I had some insight into who my brothers were. It felt strange, almost like I was spying on them because I was scrutinizing their every word, every moment, in hopes of detecting similarities and family traits that we all might share.

***

On December 15, 1999, my adoptive father, Bill, died after a decade of care and attention. It had been a long, slow decline with hospitalizations and relocations from independent living to assisted care and then to nursing care near our home in Massachusetts. He never recovered. He was eighty-nine years old. It was the end of an era. The long, special, and unforgettable moments with my adoptive father were over. He had been the best dad ever.

Bill's memorial service was held on December 18 at the St. Thomas Church in Underhill, Vermont. It was the same place where my mother, Mary, had her funeral service many years earlier. Bill's grandchildren, Jonathan, Holly, and Sean, recited readings from the

Bible and "Prayers of the Faithful," while other grandchildren, Sue (Edwards) Tatro and Kathy Edwards, delivered the offertory.

I tearfully provided a sense of Bill's love for his family and friends and what it meant to be especially close to him during the last nine years of his life. I shared many fond memories of Grandpa Luck growing up in Amsterdam, New York, near the Sassafras Woods on the Mohawk River. Bill's tales of raccoons raiding the garbage pail or the elephant in the woods no one ever saw. When they were young, Sean and Holly begged Grandpa Luck to tell the same stories over and over.

Then, I read a note Bill had written to my mother, Mary, on the back of an inspirational card after she died. The card was entitled, "For those living alone."

I love you, Mary, every day. It becomes more urgent, but I know you are where you should be with your God. I hope and strive to be with you in heaven and will keep my life holy enough to see you soon. So, keep trying to have me be the best I can be, so I'll be with you sometime soon.

Your loving husband,
Bill

It was a long ride to the cemetery. I watched Bill lowered into the ground next to my mother and little sister, Rosemary. My life with my adoptive parents had come full circle. A reception followed at our Underhill home. It was a joyous occasion as friends and family regaled each other with Bill's sense of humor, dignity, and substance. There were many funny stories. My Irish grandmother, Alice, and my mother, Mary, would have been proud.

~ 14 ~

"THIS IS MY SON"

On October 29, 1999, I took a bold step.

I felt that the time was right. My father had passed away, and time marched on. I was ready to make yet another attempt at completing the circle. I asked to meet Pat.

Dear Mr. Ward,

Our New England fall has been splendid with color, a nice affirmation of our life on earth.

[I went on to describe the expectation of a second grandchild (a girl) and how each of my three children was doing. I also shared the happy news that we had finally completed the construction of our planned retirement home in Underhill, Vermont.]

My work will bring me to San Francisco in late November. Although in the past you have expressed reluctance to meet, it would be meaningful to me to have lunch or dinner with you. It would be special to shake your hand, give you a hug, walk a bit, and share stories. I'd love to hear more about your trip to Iran in search of Hassan and his family and your past life there.

I will be staying four nights at the Beresford Arms Hotel from November 17 until Sunday morning, November 21st. I have business meetings and will host a University of Massachusetts Boston alumni event on Thursday evening, November 18, to celebrate the university's alumnus, Mabel Teng, of the San Francisco Board of Supervisors. Other times, I have meetings with prominent alumni in the area seeking their philanthropic support. However, I can juggle my schedule for any time that may be convenient for you. Would you be available for lunch or dinner on the 19th or 20th, or even an early morning breakfast on Sunday before I leave? I must leave by 11:40 a.m.

I hope we can find a way to get together. Please let me know what may work best for you. Write or e-mail me at home or work.

All best wishes to you and your family,
With warm regards,
Michael

I was pleasantly surprised to receive a rapid reply.

November 8, 1999
Dear Michael,
Breakfast on Sunday, November 21st, at the Beresford Arms Hotel sounds fine – at about 9:30 a.m. It will allow you time to make your flight without undue rush. I'll call your room when I arrive. Have a great time with your UMass Boston alums.
Fond regards,
Pat Ward

His response energized me for several reasons. First, after three years with only written correspondence and no phone calls, there was now an actual plan to meet. Second, Pat signed his letter, "Fond regards," which was an incredibly heartwarming gesture. Third, Pat was willing to see me just before I departed for the airport. Our proposed meeting certainly didn't leave much wiggle room for a lengthy meeting. I wasn't sure if Pat's requested visit time was the only time available or whether he just felt more comfortable with "distance insurance," i.e., a quick way to escape if things didn't go well. But none of that mattered because I was elated. In two weeks, I would be with my birth father for the first time.

In San Francisco, I made my way to the Beresford's Arms Hotel. With the afternoon free, I decided to see where Pat lived. I drove high into the hills of Berkeley, overlooking the Golden Gate Bridge in my rental car. Quickly glancing at the numbers on the houses flying by, I slowly passed Pat's home at 440 Spruce Street. It was built on a steep hillside with only the top story visible from the street, surrounded by a solid wooden fence that provided optimal privacy, although it offered little viewing pleasure. I wondered how many times I could drive back and forth before someone in the neighborhood might call the police. Knowing Pat was one hundred feet away stirred me. So close and yet, so far. I knew I had to be patient and wait a few more days for our scheduled visit, but I didn't have to imagine where Pat lived anymore.

Sunday, November 21, 1999, was a typically cool day in San Francisco, a splendid moment to meet a father for the first time in fifty-two years. Ironically, the day also represented my first son, Sean's, birthday. I reflected on how Rita must have felt waiting to see me several years earlier. My heart raced as I assembled small presents for Pat and magnificent flowers for Donna.

In anticipation of this special moment, I carefully shared with the hotel staff and manager my desire for a perfect setting for my meeting with Pat. The manager and staff, knowing the significance of the meeting, placed "Reserved" signs on a selected corner sofa, chair, and table for a light breakfast with coffee and juice. The front desk manager told me not to worry about anything. He'd call my room phone when my visitor arrived.

Soon, the call came. "He's here," said the hotel manager on the phone. I smiled because the phone call sounded like an Ed McMann introduction for *The Tonight Show with Johnny Carson*. I practically flew out the door once I hung up the phone. In thirty seconds, I was in the lobby with presents and flowers, as well as luggage for my trip home.

I saw a balding, gray-haired man in a blue sportscoat standing in the corner of the quaint lobby as I rounded the corner. Our eyes locked as we saw each other for the first time, and I knew that was my father. I was pleasantly surprised that he was willing to exchange hugs and kisses. Then, we each took a step back, looked at each other, and embraced again. The next few hours would be a rollercoaster of emotions.

Pat in a hushed voice said, "It's so good to finally meet you. We should have done this much sooner." I was elated!

As I studied his wizened face for the first time, I realized he had only existed in photos. Now, he was in the flesh; my dream had come true. I was with my dad. The flair of personality, voice, and manner were as I had imagined. Although, no matter how hard I tried, I couldn't spot any obvious resemblance to me other than our Romanesque noses and rosy cheeks. Pat was shorter than I had imagined. At 6'1", I towered over him. His once-chiseled face had morphed with age, and his bald head held a few wisps of white hair. He was seventy-seven, so I wondered how many more visits there might be. How many more chances would we have to make things comfortable between us?

We sat tentatively on a simple couch in the hotel lounge and traded pleasantries. Pat pummeled me with questions. "How have you been? Has your university work been successful in the past few days? How's your wife, children, and grandchildren?"

I met him question for question, both of us searching for more information to complete our mental picture of each other. It seemed disjointed, and I grew impatient with the mundane topics. I understood it was nervous excitement, but I had been waiting a long time for this moment. I'm not sure what I expected, but it was more than topical banter. As we spoke, the pace quickened. Pat became more comfortable, and the conversation took a welcome turn.

Pat told me some of the family stories and legends. He said, "You would have loved your grandmother, Grace Kelly. She had a gift of the blarney. Regularly, she told us stories about the 'little people' in Ireland and would often regale us with her childhood escapades. All of her stories began, 'Once when I was a little girl...'"

I smiled as he continued. "Your grandmother worked in Ireland as a domestic servant and was coming home from the fair on her day off when something strange happened. Your great-grandmother had given her a strict admonition. It rang in her ear: 'Be sure to get some small packets of sugar, some salt, and cakes for the rest.' The idea of 'cakes for the rest' was a magical word. Momma never forgot to add some sweets whenever she went to shop. However, on your grandmother's way home, it grew dark and gloomy. In the dense fog, she clutched the bag of treats from the fair. She had to cross a stream. With the foul weather, the stream became a raging river. She was scared and looked for a safe place to cross. Suddenly, this little fellow spoke to her through the fog: 'You'll never get across that way.' Your grandmother asked, 'Well then, where can I cross?' He gleefully exclaimed, 'If you will give me a cookie, I'll tell you.' But she was never intimidated by threats, so she spoke out and told him, 'I'll find me own way, thank you, because these cakes and cookies are for my ma.' The disgruntled little person said, 'Oh all right, come here, and I'll show you where to cross.'"

He smiled. "My mother told us this story over and over again about Ireland's little people with an ever-present twinkle in her eye, and we believed every bit of it."

Pat then shared more details about his life. "My brother, Sean (John), always built a ramshackle cabin in the backyard of every house our family ever rented. Sean was frequently despondent because we moved so often. The moves were made to take advantage of the free first month's rent. We didn't have much money. I don't think my brothers and sisters were aware of how our parents had to scrape by. Sometimes, when we had no rent money, we claimed the house was haunted. One of us would drag chains on the floor of the attic when the landlord came to collect the money. This always frightened him off. The spooky act ensured we'd get a reprieve because the hysterics always left the landlord saying he'd come back another day."

Pat then said, "I remember my brother, Jimmy, had everyone in stitches when he was younger. He made his first stage appearance when Momma insisted he recite 'I See Kitty' to her friends. He stood in the parlor to perform from his First Reader Book. However, in his innocence, he stumbled over the word 'kitty' and, instead, Momma's friends heard, 'I see Titty. Titty is in the shoe. Do you like your shoe, Titty...Titty? Titty does not say.' As you might guess, no one corrected him."

"Other days, when my poppa had a day off, he would play his fiddle music. In Donegal, Ireland, where my parents were from, music always accompanied the 'Donegal Men Dances.' In Bayonne, my father practiced using our pets as an audience. I never thought our dogs, Bingo and Trixie, and cats, Big Nuts and Little Nuts, were terribly amused. As you can imagine, Poppa had bawdy jokes about the naming of our cats, which, at the time, was totally lost on us until we were older."

Pat reminded Michael that in the Bayonne neighborhood, he and his brothers were particularly zealous about protecting their young sister, Ann Marie.

"We saw a lecherous sneer on every possible suitor's face and were determined our sister's virginal youth be insured, till old age or marriage, no matter who had to suffer. Once, when our sister came back from the beach after being away overnight, she declared she had slept in a car with some friends, including males. The sleepover was all quite innocent, but we were concerned there was 'honor' at stake. I issued the command to my brothers, 'Let's go.'

"On an early Sunday morning, we went to the boy's home. The supposed culprit was still in bed in all his innocence. We rousted him out of the sack and gave him holy hell while his distraught parents looked on in horror. Macho, sure, but not in the sleazy sense of macho in the modern world where it's packaged with neurotic violence and no spiritual substance."

My father continued with his stories, pouring them out like he'd kept them bottled up for decades or I was the only person who had not heard the tales a hundred times. "On another occasion, I saved my brothers from violence and death, so I was called 'Patty the Protector.' The label was probably the best title I ever received." Smiling, he admitted he'd been called far worse.

"One day my brothers, Jimmy and Sean, were in a fight on a hill above the bay with the neighborhood ruffians: the Broher brothers, hulking, angry, bashing types. Suddenly, I appeared out of nowhere wielding a 2 x 4 and hit one of them on the head sending him sprawling down the hill. The fight was over.

"On another day, Jimmy was sinking in freezing water after an ill-conceived winter sled ride across the bay. As the water soaked his winter clothes, dragging him down from out of the haze, I appeared with a rope to haul him to safety."

I was in tears laughing because the intriguing stories were theatrical performances that were sensitive, poignant, humorous, and undoubtedly embellished just a bit. They were Pat's way of introducing himself and his family. The gestures, change in voice, and the conjured Irish brogue made each story a revelation. I loved the fact the stories were mostly true, like any good Irish story.

It was time to jump in with my own story, although not nearly as humorous. I described my historic trip to China twenty years earlier (1982) to Pat. "After I arrived at Wayne State University (WSU)as Senior Vice President, George Romney, former Michigan Governor and Nixon-era cabinet member, was appointed to the University's Board of Governors. Nixon had successfully opened diplomatic relations with Red China. As a result, Romney worked with the U.S. State Department and Chinese officials to arrange an inaugural musical cultural exchange between WSU and China. It would be a first. Recommended as the leader for the WSU group, I helped organize the concert tour for the university's symphonic band. The Chinese were quite familiar with string instruments but not symphonic music (brass instruments). Such instruments were banned as subversive with gyrating rock and rollers. Despite the ban, many Chinese heard jazz and symphonic music played on smuggled cassette tapes."

I assembled an appropriate delegation, made the required arrangements, and acquired gifts to help pay for transportation, lodging, and food for fifty-five band members and chaperones. A Detroit travel agency facilitated the logistics for the three-week tour. My dear friend, Sue Nine, a WSU alum, convinced Detroit television station Channel 2 to accompany us and film the historic trip. The TV station sent daily news clips to the U.S. for the evening news. Our delegation consisted of Sue, her daughter Diane, several members of the University Board of Governors, a Detroit TV station news team, fifty-five student musicians, the orchestra director, Harold Arnoldi, and his wife.

"The Chinese government broadcasted each performance on the country's only television station, which was frequently watched by dozens crowding into one house. Before every performance, I stood on stage and recited my diplomatic introductory lines. Then, a young woman (government media star) would repeat what I had just said in Chinese. However, I was suspicious because there were moments during her presentation when the audience laughed, but I hadn't said anything funny. No one was ever sure exactly what she said. But, crowded into small neighborhood homes in the countryside, tens of millions of Chinese citizens witnessed symphonic music for the first time. The concert tour was a major success. Even better, the film of the triumphant symphonic band tour, assembled by the Detroit TV station crew, was nominated for an Emmy award."

Turning to Pat, I then shared the photographs I had brought with me. There was much discussion about each one. I offered my other presents to Pat along with the flowers for Donna.

The time passed too quickly, and soon, the hotel desk clerk signaled to me my airport taxi was waiting. The clerk stepped forward on cue and asked if he could take a photo of the two of us. So, with our arms around each other's shoulders, father and son, we were instantly immortalized in color. It was the only photo taken.

Spontaneously, Pat said out loud to anyone listening, "This is my son!" I was overjoyed. Those in the lobby nodded and applauded.

Teary-eyed Pat stepped closer and said, "The next time you are in town, Donna and I would like you to come to our home for dinner."

Thunderstruck, this invitation was more than I had imagined or believed would ever happen. I had sadly guessed my hotel meeting with my father might be the first and last time we'd see each other. Presuming I had passed the Pat Ward "I'm-not-sure-if- I-really-want-to-get-to- know-him" litmus test, I was thrilled. It was, after all, Pat's call. It was up to him to decide where and how our relationship might continue.

I stammered, "Thank you so much! I can't wait to see you again and meet Donna. Please give Donna the flowers and thank her for all her kindness, understanding, and warm invitation to your home."

Pat expressed appreciation for my thoughtful gifts and for urging him to establish our first meeting. He gave the impression he was genuinely pleased and happy the ice had finally been broken. There was a long embrace with furtive comments of affection. I helped Pat carry his gifts and flowers to his car and waved as he drove away.

I then went back inside the hotel to get my luggage. The desk clerk called out, "Was that really your father? You said the two of you had never met?"

I replied, "Yes, he is my birth father. We met today and embraced for the first time in five decades."

The desk clerk then quickly told me about a time when he also had found a long-lost relative. His quick story was reassuring and enhanced the sense that many families have undiscovered secrets. The refrain *don't tell anyone* echoed in my conscience as I ducked into the waiting taxi.

~ 15 ~

THE LAYERS UNFOLD

I quickly sent a note to Pat expressing my elation at our time together and my pleasure at receiving an invitation to come for dinner sometime at his house.

Characteristically, Pat responded two months later.

January 21, 2000
Dear Michael,
Just got back from a lengthy trip East. We spent Thanksgiving with the families of my brother, Sean, and my son, Chris. Then we enjoyed Christmas with son Kevin's loving entourage in their new Shelter Island home. We had a grand and festive time, but we were glad to leave the frigid weather.
I too enjoyed our get-together and I am pleased you have accomplished so much in your life. Thanks again for your thoughtful gifts and those pictures came out well from the impressed roving photographer.
Enclosed is my Christmas note now that I have your address at hand.
Fondest regards,
Pat

Pat's 2000 Ward Family Christmas Letter described the thrill of maneuvering an invitation to be in the NYC St. Patrick's Day Parade with his sons. It was a moment to celebrate his long-standing membership with the National Irish Aid (NIA) organization. Historically, the NIA gave financial assistance and other services to the widows, wives, and children of fallen or incarcerated members of the Irish Republican Army (IRA). With drums and bagpipes playing, Pat gathered under the NIA banner with sons Kevin, Chris, Richard, and Terry. They marched up Fifth Avenue from 41st Street to 86th Street. They held banners inscribed, "Support the Good Friday Agreement" and "Free All Irish POWs." Amid snow flurries, there were cheers and clapping. Pat suggested the experience was "pure magic."

***

The time arrived when I could accept Pat's invitation for a visit to see him and meet his wife, Donna, at their Berkeley home. Barbara and I had planned a visit to the West Coast to see Holly, who was teaching in Pasadena, and I asked Pat if all of us would accept his invitation for dinner around that time.

Pat replied.

August 18, 2000
Dear Michael,
Donna and I will be delighted to meet with you, Barbara, and Holly for lunch at our home in Berkeley. We finally managed to keep the time over the Labor Day weekend free for the occasion. Give me a call when you're settled in San Francisco, and we will work out a time and day.

By the way, congratulations on your son Jonathan's admittance to Mary Washington College in Virginia. It's a fine school, and he'll be relatively close to home for visits, which is a plus. From his record he must be an exemplary boy.

Warm regards,
Patrick

The day after arriving at Holly's home in Pasadena, we soon all boarded a flight to Oakland to go to Pat's home. This meeting would be a first for Barbara and Holly. We greeted them with flowers and warm introductions. Holly, ever the observer, took in every detail. Similar to meeting Rita for the first time, expectations were modified and adjusted. Everyone was on their best behavior. Donna was tender and warm, and Pat, his usual engaging self, toured his steep backyard filled with fruit trees.

Growing closer with Pat involved conversations about personal and tangential things. Pat reveled in his love for family and all those around him. I reminded him that he had a new great granddaughter, Kathryn Rachel Luck, born on February 17 and that his great grandson, Patrick Ryan Luck, was now four years old.

Donna was an extraordinary cook, preparing and serving an outstanding meal for us to relish. We were joined for dinner by Pat's sister Anne-Marie and her daughters, Susan and Kristen. It felt like a new beginning, although I wondered why Pat was comfortable with his sister and his nieces knowing of my existence but not his sons, but I didn't ask.

After returning to Boston, we sent a letter of appreciation to Pat and Donna.

Dear Donna and Patrick,

Home again, home again, jiggety jig!

It's hard to transcend time and space so quickly. So, it is, being home again after such a truly wonderful time in California. I think we left our hearts and minds suspended there, full of feeling and excitement in having discovered such kindred spirits in the two of you. Thank you so much for your warm and gracious hospitality! We all enjoyed every minute of our time with you.

It occurred to me that the art of letter writing is a deep and common thread between you and your boys. Perhaps storytelling is the best way to communicate with them about the existence of Michael. Perhaps you might consider sending a letter to all four boys. Naturally, the story would be enhanced by referencing that Michael's debut took place fifty-three years ago. Of course, the whole saga is wrenching because of Rita's self-proclaimed "foolish pride."

We shall call as soon as I know it is your preferred way to communicate.

Thank you both. We were overjoyed with our time spent sharing and learning from you and holding memories dear. We hope we can pick up the thread in the not-too-distant future.
With great affection,
Barbara and Michael

In subsequent letters, Pat spoke about the good things in his life. Then, abruptly, the tone of his communication changed. He said he was having a hard time because Donna was not feeling well. We expressed concern and asked if there was anything we could do. Soon, Pat's news brought greater sadness. Donna had been diagnosed with cancer. This was devastating to us. It was clear Pat depended on Donna to steer the ship while he stood on the bow waving his sword and demanding bravery from everyone.

Barbara dashed off a letter right away.

February 6, 2002
Dear Pat and Donna,
Michael and I experienced a mixture of shock and delight to receive your New Year's message. It is always a delight to hear from you, Patrick. You have a marvelous affective expression, which makes us take notice of the moments we experience in the world around us. We felt connected with your daily moments, breathing, reflecting, and investing time with your beloved Donna.

Where do we begin to put to words our feelings about Donna's terminal cancer news? We sat in stunned silence for a while. With time our feelings rose up, tears welled up in our eyes as we felt the sadness of anticipated loss. The truth is we suffer apart from you. Our instincts tell us we "want to do something." We wish to contribute in some way to help. The daily moments of work and chores are banal by contrast. Michael and I wish there were a way for us to call you, to be in touch, to be kept up to the minute, to know when a terrible moment happens there is a way for us to know right away. This is awkward, but constructive, too.

I am remembering our time with you and Donna in your Berkeley home last August. Since I first met Donna, I felt enormous comfort and reward from her warmth and presence. While we were with you it became second nature to enter your home, turn left and go into action with Donna in the kitchen. It was so wonderful to walk through all of your amazing gardens while deliberating the world around us. I must admit in the dreadful moment of our shock and silence I said to Michael, "Donna is exactly the person and friend I had hoped my mother would have been to me."

Michael said, "You need to tell her."

We need to take courage in the moment. Courage for us is in the form of standing by, although we would jump on a plane in a heartbeat for the opportunity to visit, give you both a hug, and sip some tea together, nothing more or less. Let us know if you could squeeze us in anytime. We would love to come.

We offer you support and strength on your journey together. We hope to hear a word or two or sit together without any.

With special love,
Barbara and Michael

***

Donna died a year later on March 25, 2003. A celebration of her life was planned at their Berkeley home. Pat struggled with the right words:

"Our beloved Donna gave up her struggle with breast cancer. Coincidentally, the date she died was the anniversary of our marriage fifty-three years ago when she was a sweet nineteen-year-old bride in Boulder, Colorado. She went gently into the night with a beautiful, blissful smile on her lovely face attended by her four sons and me at her bedside.

"Prior to her leaving we had taken turns talking softly into her ear affirming our undying love which she acknowledged by pressing on clasped fingers. It was grief personified fading into a beautiful peacefulness. There would be no more pain and gasping for breath or dealing with the needles and tubes which she abhorred. It was all so quiet.

"Donna, my angel, had more than fulfilled her mission on Earth. Because I'm convinced the Supreme Creator of all things sends a special emissary on Earth to act as a model of goodness and compassion for the rest of us to follow. Donna was the chosen saint, and hopefully, there is an infant out there selected to take her place.

"Donna started on her compassionate concern for all creatures at the age of five. In Kansas, spring hail stones could (and did) knock baby birds out of their nests. Donna would carefully collect them for her 'Birdie Hospital,' a large box with soft down, and nurse them until they would fly away. She seldom lost one. She continued to apply the same compassionate assistance to all she met who needed special care.

"There are numerous stories of miraculous happenings brought about by her intervention. She never expected personal aggrandizement or gratitude. It was on to the next project of another wounded bird needing to fly."

On March 29th (her 73rd birthday) Pat and his sons had a gala memorial at their home to celebrate Donna's life for family and dear friends. They recited poems composed for her; the children sang acapella musical tributes to their grandma and everyone shared personal and funny stories. It was a poignant and beautiful send off.

Donna's presence could be felt throughout the warm and sunny day, and I'm sure she would have enjoyed every minute. Her presence was paramount when the feasting began into the night, as we all recounted memories and stories about how Donna touched the many lives of those present.

Pat said, "Now it's healing time, and she wouldn't want us to cry, although the tears are hard to hold back at times. So, here's to our precious girl — devoted wife, consummate mom, and mother to the world. Her physical presence is gone but her spirit, love, and compassion will live on in all who knew her, now and always. Good night, my angel — you'll be with us forever with a kiss from your loving husband, Pat, and your four loving sons, Kevin, Terry, Chris, and Richard."

Pat described his heart in a fitting, but uncharacteristic manner. He clearly needed time to sort out his life without Donna. Pat spent several months traveling between his four sons. When he finally returned to California, Barbara and I traveled to see him.

Dear Pat,

Michael and I have had so many wonderful moments reflecting upon the special time we shared with you in Berkeley. Your hospitality was exceptionally generous! I mentioned a few times in all sincerity attending theatrical productions is Michael's idea of nirvana! So indeed, the schedule you planned for us was particularly wonderful. In addition to stimulating our sensibilities and imagination, it was wonderful to enjoy the different theaters. The one in Orinda was reminiscent of the Acropolis Theater in Athens. It had a feeling of the Greek theater. The production was well done with the two outstanding female performers. Wrapped in a blanket and out in the fresh air, my senses all came alive! It was the first night in many that I had been able to relax and be receptive to everything outside of myself. It was wonderful!

The two other plays integrated well into our unfolding moments together. A well-done, humorous, and energetic show, Pirates of Penzance invigorated all of us with the power of bucking the system!

We'll see each other again soon.

~ 16 ~

ANOTHER DOOR OPENS

On June 6, 2003, Barbara and I gathered family and friends at our home in Vermont, where the stage was set for our 25th anniversary and son Jonathan's 21st birthday.

The celebration unfolded on the lawn. The day's fierce wind and threatening rain made our billowing white tent a welcome refuge. Fireworks, a family favorite tradition, were prepared for later in the evening if the weather cooperated.

Our homegrown family band of musicians Jonathan, Sean, and Holly, friends Sara and Chris, aka "The Underhill Revolution," were feverishly rehearsing several popular rock 'n' roll cover songs to perform as part of the festivities. New York City friends, including rock legend Ian Lloyd ("Brother Louie"), his son David, and his Social Hero band members, were graciously ready to jump on our makeshift stage after the "The Underhill Revolution" performance.

Throughout the day, my mind wandered to how nice it would have been to include Pat and the Ward brothers in our celebration. After Donna died in March, we tried unsuccessfully to reach Pat and decided to anonymously reach out to one of Pat's sons. Inside Pat's last "Ward Family Christmas" letter he revealed one son's e-mail address. So, we e-mailed brother Terry, posing as old acquaintances of his parents, and inquired about Pat's location.

May 20, 2003

Dear Terry,

We have not had a chance to meet, but we know your parents. We still mourn the recent loss of your mother. We also extend our heartfelt sympathy.

We have been unsuccessful in trying to reach your father. The last we knew, he was traveling to stay with each of his boys. It is good he can do this and have support during this most difficult time.

The last time we visited with Donna in Berkeley, we discussed a wide swath of topics, including Pat's grandparents. We asked when your Grandfather, Patrick Ward (father and son with the same name), died and where? Your mother wasn't sure, but she was going to find out. Soon, she became ill, and we chose not to bother her about it again. We were going to make a family memento for your parents. By any chance, do you know how best to reach Pat? We would be most appreciative.

Again, please accept our deepest sympathy.

Barbara C. Wilson and Michael F. Luck

We received no communication. So, we tried a different tactic. The date for Donna's memorial service was set for the Ward home in Berkeley. Immediate family, "borrowed children," and friends were requested to gather to mourn and celebrate her life. This was an opportunity to call Pat and express our deepest sympathies to him and the family.

As expected, the Ward brothers took turns fending phone calls of condolence. Barbara called, posing as Donna and Pat's friend, and to remain anonymous to their sons. Pat's oldest son, Kevin, answered the phone. He was clearly heartbroken. Barbara explained we were old friends and wanted to express our heartfelt sympathy. It was an awkward moment. We couldn't have forgiven ourselves if we had not respectfully communicated from the bottom of our hearts. Barbara asked Kevin if it would be possible to speak to Pat briefly.

Kevin said, "Dad's not taking calls at the moment. Would you be willing to call back at another time?"

Kevin promised to relay our loving sympathies to Pat and we promised to call back at a more convenient time. When Kevin ended the call and was hanging up, we heard brother Terry ask, "Who called?"

***

In Vermont, everything was ready for our anniversary festivities. Unceremoniously, a few hours before everyone's arrival, I checked my e-mail to see if there were last-minute messages from intended guests. It was completely uncanny that within a split second before shutting my computer down, the lilting sound of "You've got mail!" brought a message from Brother Terry. I had to catch my breath before I could read it. What news would it contain? This first communication with a brother might be the key to a future relationship with three others! I never had a brother so this could be quite a new experience. What would it be like to be one of five, a veritable team of testosterone?

Dear Barbara and Michael,
How wonderful to see your e-mail, our first direct contact, and receive your telephone call inquiring about Dad and my mother's memorial service here in Berkeley.
I know who you are, dear brother.
I must share with you what happened. Our mother decided to travel to Ireland for a last-ditch effort cancer cure, which was doubtful and unsuccessful. We all took turns being with her. One day, not long ago, when a soft rain fell lightly, my mother called me to her bedside. She spoke fondly of you both:
Terence, you know I am dying, and I have something to tell you, but you must keep it a secret. When you think the time is right, you must determine how best to transmit this secret to your brothers and the rest of the family.

Then, she handed me the letter you wrote to Pat several years earlier. I read the letter carefully, looking in my mother's eyes as each page unveiled a new truth. Then, my mother continued:

The letter means you have a fifth brother named Michael. He came into this world and was adopted several years before Pat and I met at the university. His mother's name is Rita, and your brother has had a wonderful relationship with her since finding her in 1994. Pat and I have quietly known him and his family for more than six years. Your father wanted to keep the existence of Michael a secret because he felt it would be too disruptive to try to fold him into the Ward clan.

When Michael reached out to your father more than five years ago, in 1998, he was uncomfortable with how to manage this piece of startling news. To be certain of his paternity, your father insisted everyone involved take a DNA test. Michael agreed and made the arrangements for the blood test at Mass General in Boston. Pat, Rita, and Michael all submitted blood samples. The test results were a positive match. There were no other possible fathers for Michael than Pat.

The news was startling at our late stage in life. Your father was in shock. I think he was certain the paternity test would exonerate him, of course, it didn't and now, your father and I had a surprise son. I felt he should be a part of our family. I suggested Pat introduce Michael to you, your brothers, and the rest of the Wards. He refused to consider such an action. Reluctantly, I respected his wishes.

So, my dear son, I am leaving the responsibility solely to you to make things right. You need to find a time when such an announcement might be best. It cannot stay a secret! Michael should be considered part of our family.

Will you do this for me?

Taking a deep breath, I tried to evaluate what I had just read. It was clear Terry had accepted Donna's request. I wondered why she had selected him for this task. Was she running out of time and wanted to be sure someone knew the "secret?" Did she think Terry might be the best messenger to handle the delicate timing of such remarkable news? Then, again, maybe Terry was simply the last one in the door? Only posterity knows the answer. But Terry made a promise to his mother, and he intended to keep it.

Terry's e-mail message continued:

It was a month before the family, including Donna, returned from Ireland to Berkeley, where she had undergone some controversial therapies she hoped might cure her cancer. They didn't.

Days later, Donna took her last breath and we plunged into the delicate role of caring for Pat, so alone mapping out his inner landscapes so emptied from such a sudden departure. We are still in shock, and at least Donna did not suffer greatly, thank God. She fought like a tiger as her shortness of breath increased, and the cancer took over. True to form, she wanted to open a new path with her journey by rejecting chemotherapy so her experience would serve as an alternative way to save others in the future without pain. In her selfless way, even then, she was only thinking about being in service to others.

My wife, Idanna, and I are now in Florence, exhausted after our long journey. Our loss of my dear mother marked a revolution in our lives, a time of complete change. We plan to make our base here. We are healing because of unexpected blessings. With Donna's death, previously hidden doors have been opened to many sensitive, illuminated souls, as well as new and recovered friendships across the country, including the two of you. We know Donna had a special hand in this gift and even now continues to guide us forward.

We are fixing up an apartment for Pat adjacent to our place in Florence. Currently, Pat is in Leiden with Rich and his family. Rich got promoted to a senior position at Shell Oil Company with responsibility for helping to map out the company's environmental direction. He was among twenty being interviewed just before he came to Berkeley to be at Mom's side. Rich said, 'Mom's working overtime.' Pat will help coach Rich during the start of his elevated job. He knows Rich can sometimes be impulsive, stubborn, and occasionally unaware of the need for peripheral vision. All this is good news because Pat wants to feel needed, and this is a perfect start. He is doing what Donna would do, riding to the rescue and being of service to loved ones. He will also help edit Rich's wife, Ellen's, master's thesis.

I will keep you abreast of Pat's movements. He will probably be with us during this summer. As to your other question, to the best of my knowledge, Patrick Sr. is buried in New Jersey with his wife, Grace Kelly. I never remembered seeing him. He passed away far too early. All the other family members are buried in Donegal, Ireland, in a plot close to Burtonport on the far west coast. The family's cottage is still there, hugging the Atlantic coast occupied by our great Aunt Susie Boyle. Pat confessed to me after spending three long months in Killaloe, County Clare, for Donna's cancer treatments, he also wants to be laid to rest in the family plot. Dad wanted his ashes someday to be mixed with Donna's, but she nixed the idea of being buried in Ireland. Idanna and I are not big fans of scattering ashes in mountains and oceans. We believe a sacred resting point of reference is so important. A suitable spot will be found.

All this is to say, we carry on in this life of extreme wonder. We will stay close to Patrick keeping bonds of love unbreakable and firm. Soon, I will tell him we four are in contact and this was Donna's wish. Her revelation about you was a tender and intimate moment and the time comes soon to heal the bonds which have been left suspended for years.

Your brother and sister,
Terence Ward and Idanna Pucci

Terry then sent another poetic message capturing his bedside meeting with his mother.

On the Shannon lies a small village of Killaloe,
Where she told me.
At first, I could not understand my mother's voice.
Mystery lay in her words.
"Take this letter from Michael Luck and read," she said.
Scanning the page, I could not decipher the meaning.
"Who wrote this?" I asked looking up.

She told me: "Terry, you have an older brother."
My mind raced as she smiled and said,
"Here, keep it. When the time comes you will know what to do."
I folded it carefully and we went back to the struggle at hand.
Over the weeks, missteps and false hopes drained us.
She was clearly leaving her body,
Which no longer could hold her.
Months passed.
She flew away.
Seasons changed.
Until one day, I returned to the letter passed to me by her hands.
When her breath trembled.
I knew it was time to open the door.
It was time to welcome old truths, as old friends.
As one leaves, another returns.
It was time to be moved.
To greet a new brother.
With much love on your 60th Birthday, Brother Michael.
Terence

Oh my, how these words and poetic verse settled over me, penetrating deep into my soul. There was such serendipity in the moment, a concurrence between the life lived and a life not yet lived, a feeling of inspiration in what the future might hold. Terry's words and verse were received seemingly as those of my own since I, too, express sentimental life transitions in a similar way. I felt greatly relieved, full of excitement, and ready for the moment that stood boldly before me.

Terry proposed a meeting so we could get to know one another and perhaps discuss how best to fulfill his mother's larger wishes. He mentioned he and Idanna intended to travel from Florence to New York City in a few months for business. They had meetings with book editors as well as a few speaking engagements, but would it be possible to meet with us in the city? This was momentous news. At that time, Barbara and I lived outside of Albany, New York, and we knew it would be an easy trip to the city for this hopeful first meeting.

Terry and Idanna would stay in their studio apartment located at the NAC on 19th Street, and we would find a place nearby. If this plan all worked, he proposed we meet at the NAC on December 1st at 5 p.m. under the stained-glass dome in the bar. How exciting and fulfilling. This was going to be a dazzling moment. Pat's long-kept secret would begin to unfold before us. It felt like I had discovered another puzzle piece. The most difficult part of Terry's invitation was having to wait so long (almost four months) to hug him as well as my sister-in-law, Idanna.

My reply was, "Absolutely, we'll see you in December!"

A New Beginning

~ 17 ~

THE FIFTH SON

It was December 1, 2003, the day I would meet my brother, Terence Ward.

Barbara and I left early from our work at The State University of New York, braced by the cold air, and raced hurriedly to the train for New York City. We were excited because it all seemed surreal. On this day, now six years after my first communication with my birth father, Pat, I felt nervous jitters but also confident our meeting would go well.

We arrived at the National Arts Club promptly at 5:00 p.m. and explained to the front desk concierge we were there to meet brother, Terence, and Idanna, at the bar.

The concierge graciously responded, "Yes, Terry told me he was expecting you. I will call and let him know you have arrived. In the meantime, please proceed up the stairs and turn right to enter the salon. You will see the bar on the far side. He will meet you there."

Barbara and I checked our coats and climbed the red-carpeted marble stairs. With pounding hearts, we marveled at such a magnificent place, founded in 1898 by author and poet Charles De Kay, the literary critic for the *New York Times*. The interior, decorated in Victorian motif, had backlit stain glass panels by John LaFarge, elaborate fireplace surrounds by Ellin & Kitson, windows heavy with drapery, and walls appropriately festooned with well-curated paintings. We learned the private club was unusual for at its inception because it admitted women on a full and equal basis. The NAC, located in the Samuel Tilden Mansion, built in the 1840s, was a National Historic Landmark.

We walked into the salon and marveled at David MacDonald's famed stained-glass dome, precisely placed above the club's bar. This location was spectacular and simply exquisite for a first meeting with a brother. Incredible!

The bartender unexpectedly queried, "Are you Terry's brother, Michael? Terry suggested I should be expecting you today. You're his long-lost brother, right?"

I nodded. The bartender continued. "This will be quite an evening. While you're waiting, what can I get for you?"

With a drink in hand and feelings of apprehension, I reminded myself that first impressions count. We were both wearing business attire, which seemed appropriate. What would Terry think of us? What would Terry and Idanna be like? Did Terry already have a plan to reveal my existence to his other brothers? How would Terry tell Pat about his mother's message insisting I be folded into the family?

No sooner had I taken the first sip of my drink when Terry appeared in the arched doorway to the bar. Red hair swept back, ruddy cheeks, blue eyes, and a big smile on his face, he approached us with a grand sweeping Irish welcome of embraces and kisses.

"Hey, my brother Michael, it is so good to finally meet you as well as Barbara."

Terry's style was elegant with an extraverted exuberance like his father. It crossed my mind how much Terry looked like he did in the "Ward Brothers Iran" video, but I didn't say anything.

Terry quickly announced that Idanna would soon arrive; she was running late rescheduling a meeting with her book editor. I suspected she may have wanted Terry to have a private moment with Barbara and me before she arrived. Everyone's facial expressions suggested there was much to be learned from this first meeting.

Terry was undoubtedly sizing me up and wondering how I would fit into the family.

Soon, Idanna arrived in a flourish, greeting us enthusiastically. A classic beauty, she expressed a warm smile and gentle manner. She suggested we all sit in the salon for a cocktail before dinner. It seemed like an auspicious beginning.

The next hour, saturated with multiple conversations, jumped from one topic to another in an easy flow. It was a question-and-answer marathon. Both Idanna and Terry were characteristically engaging, although there were moments when I felt like I was trying to ace a job interview only to be told it went to someone else. This personal encounter felt a little like a trial run. Their assessment of our meeting would undoubtedly color the rest of the story.

Over a sumptuous dinner, Terry asked, "Would the two of you be able to attend the UN presentation I'm making tomorrow?" He was scheduled to speak to a group of global NGOs about tactics to understand and achieve peace in the Middle East, particularly in Iran. Terry's invitation would give us a chance to spend more time together.

I immediately responded, "Sure."

Barbara wasn't able to join us. As the Assistant for Presidential Searches and Evaluation to the Chancellor of the State University of New York (SUNY), she had to be in Albany the next day for a planned board meeting.

It seemed like Terry's invitation was a sign our first meeting was going well. The event would give me a chance to see him in action. It might be revelatory. Terry assured me my name would be on a UN list to ensure entrance through their extensive security system. The evening closed with warm hugs and expressions of great joy. It seemed like a half-century of absence faded.

The next morning, I quickly entered the UN building and made my way to the location of Terry's presentation. Several dozen NGOs had already assembled. Terry was sitting by himself, making last-minute notes. He looked up and warmly greeted me, "Hey, brother,

I am so pleased you're here. How did you sleep last night? I don't know about you, but I was awake thinking about our time together and trying to integrate it all. Sometimes, it felt like my emotional bank account was overdrawn. I have concluded this idea of a new brother is exciting."

I smiled and said, "I feel the same way and I am thrilled to be attending your presentation."

Within minutes, Terry was giving his speech about his experience growing up in Iran and the implications for a better understanding of the Middle East. He was methodical, articulate, and knowledgeable in a way that encouraged attendees to lean in so they could hear his words. It was a pleasure for me to see the reaction of the audience to Terry's presentation.

When Terry concluded, we chatted briefly before saying goodbye. I told him I loved him and, of course, his presentation. Making that affectionate comment surprised me, as it just slipped out, but it was the way I felt at the moment.

I was pleasantly moved when Terry said, "I love you, too, brother."

He suggested he would reveal my existence as a fifth Ward brother at a strategic moment in the future. He wasn't sure of the timing, but he would figure out how best to do it. I understood completely and sensed Terry wanted to be cautious with the idea of introducing a new brother. I certainly couldn't fault him for that. Some family members might be more receptive to the news than others. At that moment, I felt a connection with Terry beyond just a long-lost half-brother. A new chapter was unfolding for me at fifty-six years old.

Soon after meeting Terry and Idanna, Barbara wrote a lengthy letter with photos so they might better understand the full context of our lives.

Dear Terry and Idanna,

Greetings and felicitations to you both! I imagine your summer is taking on a rhythm and structure with a focus on writing that will eventually be shrouded with great affection and satisfaction. However, at the moment hot days and long hours may be twisting your well-developed articulation into moments of brilliance and others of silence. The heart and soul are revitalized through the process, which I expect provides great satisfaction and rewards. Please know we are thinking of you at this time.

Over the past couple of weeks, I found some time to put photos in albums. With the celebrations at the end of May, Father's Day, Fourth of July weekend, etc., we have enjoyed many hours of family and friend time. While at work on these projects I selected a variety of photos of our clan. They aren't the best photos of us, and all of us would rather think we are much "better looking" in real life, but they don't lie! I made four copies of these photos for such time when you would like to share our story with your brothers. I scanned enormous quantities of photos into my computer only to find that every time I try to send one, it is returned. Thus, this stop-gap measure to share with you images of us and our lives.

The first set of photos is of Michael and me, taken during our family festivities in May. Michael has a grandson, Patrick Luck, on his lap at a time way past his bedtime. He is a sweet six-year-old, bright, and serious with an artistic talent like his father, Michael's son, Sean. He enters first grade in the fall. This summer, he and Sean are designing and building a tree house in Mendon, Massachusetts, where they live. Both seem to enjoy the process enormously. The photo of Michael and me was taken at the conclusion of our festivities. The one of Michael outside our Vermont home, I believe, was taken a few weeks later when the warm glow of the sun cast its light across our lawn. Michael loves sitting outside in that spot to read the newspaper or relax at the end of the day. The light is nice, and you can see he looks relaxed and comfortable in the photo.

The next set is of Sean and Patrick. This photo was taken at the anniversary/birthday party after Sean (36) and the other family members performed for the first time as a rock 'n' roll band calling themselves 'The Underhill Revolution.' Patrick is the aspiring Rocker! On Sunday morning after our party, Sean and his wife, Gail, cooked up breakfast for the slow-moving "morning after" revelers. The last shot is of Patrick, taken Christmas 2002.

Sean and Gail are our computer technological experts. Sean graduated from Worcester Polytechnic Institute in computer science and electrical engineering. He first worked as an applications engineer at Cognex. Then, he moved on to digital equipment, where he gained a lot of experience in preparation for management. He worked as a manager at Parametric Technology for several years before becoming chief technology officer at Smart Routes. From there he worked for two venture capital companies engaged in transportation issues. At the moment, he is working on the idea of starting his own company called Route Watch. The concept is to provide the software in support of transportation needs, i.e., to serve the individual consumer with navigational systems built into new cars and the government for transportation and movement of equipment, etc. Gail graduated from Bates in Physics with a minor in computer science. She has worked at Analog Devices for over a decade, starting as a systems analyst, and has worked her way up to project manager.

The next set of photos includes Sean's wife, Gail, and our granddaughter, Katie, age three. The picture of Katie with her mother was taken a year ago when they were with us for Father's Day, 2002. The other two show her "style" and delight over party involvement! Katie is extremely bright, running circles around most of us, and definitely keeps us all on our toes and on edge!

Daughter Holly (32), married Chris Knight (32) on November 11, 2001, at an Elvis Chapel in Las Vegas. It was lots of fun and representative of their shared passion for "Rock 'n' Roll." Chris is from L.A. and played for a number of years as a professional drummer. You see him here at our Albany home, pool reflected in the background. Chris and Holly just moved from the Boston area to Burlington, Vermont. Chris is working as a cook for a prominent restaurant in downtown Burlington. Holly is a master's prepared elementary school teacher. She has taught 5/6 grade, 5th grade, 3rd grade, and Montessori. She just landed a position in Burlington designing curriculum and working as a lead teacher in a preschool. She has a real gift for working with children.

For more than eleven years (1966-1977) Michael was married to Sean and Holly's mother, Barbara Benzie. After their 1978 divorce, Barbara also remarried and has a daughter, Maria, (22) from that marriage. Unfortunately, her marriage did not survive. Presently, she lives in the D.C. area, working as a paralegal.

Michael grew up in Burlington, Vermont. His father, Bill Luck, was the head of the IRS for the State of Vermont. His mother, Mary Leddy Luck, was a masters trained teacher who taught English for years. She was born on a farm in Underhill, close to where our present VT home is located. The Leddy family is community-minded. Uncle Bernard ran for governor (lost by 400 votes), Cousin Jimmy Leddy is a VT state senator and his sister, Joey Donovan, a state representative. They are great people dedicated to human welfare. Michael's best childhood friend, Bill Sorrell, is Vermont Attorney General. So, Michael got his political bearings as a young man!

Michael spent all his summers in Underhill fishing, hiking, and playing imaginary games in the country. His sister, Nancy Edwards, is eleven years older than he is, and his younger sister, Rosemary, died at the age of four of cystic fibrosis. All three were adopted from Catholic Social Services.

Michael is amazing! He has exceptional abilities to concentrate and get things done. Having been blessed with the Ward performance gene, he regularly tackles workshop presentations, speeches, and the details of event planning with creativity and exceptional attention to detail. He understands how to communicate. His portfolio includes campaign case statements, award-winning campus films, and topnotch marketing materials. He has been in senior management of colleges, universities, and hospitals for over thirty years.

Michael became a father at age nineteen. This precluded his having a parallel college experience to most of us, but clearly motivated him to apply his natural abilities to achieve personal goals. With his talents, Michael blasted through college while working to support his small family. It was a real honor that his undergraduate college, Johnson State College, just awarded him the "Distinguished Alumnus of the Year" Award.

Accepted into graduate school in Anthropology at Cornell and Southern Illinois University, Michael went to SIU (they offered an assistantship). In four years, he emerged with an Anthropology Masters and Higher Education Administration Doctorate. As a member of the Vietnam generation, he did his part serving in the National Guard, retiring as captain after twelve years. He has many stories to share that the children still beg him to tell any inner circle newcomer.

Michael never imagined he would become a superior, professional fundraiser. However, there is a good connection between his devotion to Anthropology and fundraising. He focuses on an individual's desire to give back as part of kinship traditions. Thirty years later, he can boast a landmark book on community college development and personal oversight of more than $1 billion raised to support hospitals and higher education. Naturally, his favorite community activity was as chair of a regional theater board in Allentown, Pennsylvania. Through all of his work, he formed lifelong relationships, which gave him a rich and rewarding life. His work provides much value to individuals, institutions, and communities.

In 1982, Michael and I welcomed Jonathan into the world four years after we were married. In these photos, you see Jonathan (age 20) on the cable car in San Francisco during our visit with Patrick and Donna last year. More recently you see him at his grandmother (Michael's biological mother), Rita Mills', 76th birthday and at our home in Albany. He is 21, 6'7" tall, a sensitive and gentle young man with a keen mind and insatiable intellectual curiosity. When he graduated from Wayland High School (MA), the faculty bestowed upon him the "Frank Smith Award" as the Renaissance Man of his class. He is motivated by the arts (art history, music, literature, with a special interest in post-modernism and film), a passion he has pursued concurrently with his undergraduate studies in philosophy. At present, he is struggling with the unwieldy questions associated with the next steps in his life. As of today, it looks as if he might pursue a master's in counseling while enjoying the Writer's Institute here at UAlbany.

In some ways, Jonathan is much like my brother, Paul Wilson, who studied English at Harvard. He then went on to study at Trinity College, Cambridge only to decide to change his focus to art history. Eventually, he pursued a doctorate in English at UVA. He remains knowledgeable and interested in the arts, much the same as Jonathan. However, the more I hear about Terry's interests and intellectual pursuits, the more I imagine Jonathan reflects parallel interests and passions.

Next, you will see poster photos of the "Underhill Revolution." Sean, Holly, and Jonathan played at our 25th wedding anniversary party when Michael received his first communication from you. They were terrific!

Finally, I include pictures of our home in Underhill, Vermont. In 1947, Bill Luck built a small camp at the base of Mt. Mansfield, where the family spent summers throughout Michael's childhood. As the family grew, we all came to love this spot in the mountains. Many a good time was spent fishing, mountain climbing, swimming in the mountain streams, and generally enjoying the country.

Wherever we were living (New Jersey, Michigan, Pennsylvania, Texas, or Massachusetts), Michael and I returned each summer for a visit to Underhill. When Michael's parents passed away, we held onto the summer camp for a few years until a larger tract of land became available up the road. About five years ago, we began construction on a new weekend/retirement home, which is what you see in the pictures. Stowe is on the other side of Mt. Mansfield from our house. Our home is located on the highest road traversing the mountain below state-owned land. We have marvelous views and absolute privacy. The location is close to skiing, Burlington, and Lake Champlain for summer water activities. Our neighbors are wonderful people who add a lot to our feeling of well-being when we are there. Little by little, we are landscaping. The trees you see in blossom were planted a year ago.

To our surprise, our interest in using old wood (roofer board, 150-year-old pine, and chestnut from farmhouses and schools) in a new home generated much attention, so much so two articles were written about our home. One was published in the Burlington Free Press (1999), the other on the cover of the real estate section of the NY Times Millennium edition, January 2, 2000! Subsequent to that article, artist friend Ray Sauer completed an original three-dimensional bronze and steel, square stock sculpted stair railing for the house. He did a remarkable job. It adds incredible aesthetic value to the house. Michael and I consider ourselves fortunate to have had the opportunity to work with amazing artists throughout the whole building project. The grandchildren call the house "Grandpa's Castle."

This summer, Jonathan was living in our Vermont home until recently when he moved back to Albany. These days we spend weekends and holidays there until such time we retire. Then, we expect to split our year between Vermont (summer and fall) and (winter/spring) Southern Europe: Spain, France, or Italy. I have close connections to Spain through my former husband, Luis Valls, who lives in Valencia. I spent most of my twenties living in Europe, primarily Germany and Spain, with the good fortune to drop in at my parents' Provencal home, located near Bandol in the village of Le Beausset. My mother was English and raised in London, giving me family ties there. More recently, we have spent time in Italy, thus the Mediterranean spread for our prospective winter retreat.

Because of my parents' activities, at an early age, I was exposed to international travel and foreign languages. Michael and I have tried to offer Jonathan similar opportunities. A few years ago, he spent five weeks in Florence studying art restoration with a friend of mine, Bette Tomberli. She is an artist who works on restoration for the Uffizi and Pitti galleries. Bette is a marvelous resource and was able to take Jonathan behind the scenes at the Piazza Signoria, where he learned not only about the restoration process but also the associated politics involved in restoration work. For all that time, Jonathan lived in a small room at a hotel in the center of Florence. On his days off from Bette's tutorials, he spent time at the British Library, which I understand is close to you on the Via dei Bardi. We also have a lifelong family friend who lives in a beautiful villa in Fiesole, whom Jonathan was able to visit often. Naturally, as a result of this experience, Jonathan fell in love with Florence and Italy.

Last but not least, I'll tell you about myself. Growing up, our homestead in Seekonk, Massachusetts, was a well-established gentleman's farm (1795). My mother, a great horse enthusiast, founded the New Forest Pony Association of North America. Throughout her life we had anywhere from ten to twenty ponies and horses, even entertaining a riding school for a number of years. I am the youngest of four, with two older sisters and an older brother. As a child, I was fortunate to travel across Europe, spending long summers on a farm in Wales; at sixteen, traveling across Europe visiting the Ministers of Science with my parents, and at seventeen, accompanied by a girlfriend, exploring London and its environs. This was the foundation for future travels in Europe and my express comfort on that continent.

European travel was common due to my father, Carroll Wilson's work at MIT and the UN. Beginning in 1959 my father became a professor at MIT after a short career in industry preceded by government work, beginning before WWII. During the war, he worked closely with the OSRD and Vannevar Bush. Right after the War (1947-1950), he served as the first general manager of the Atomic Energy Commission. Later, my father's work as chairman of the OECD Scientific Research Committee placed him in either Paris or Geneva for meetings. During this time, he found the wonderful community of Le Beausset, France, and built a small home.

In 1970, my father participated in the Study of Critical Environmental Problems (SCEP) and, in 1971, the Study of Man's Impact on Climate (SMIC). He was so motivated by climate and environmental issues that he spent the next ten years of his life chairing global energy studies. In fact, Shell Oil in the Netherlands had a representative participant on the Workshop for Alternative Energy Strategies, a project which concluded in 1977. Along the way, my father became a member of the Executive Committee of the Club of Rome as the result of his collaboration with Jay Forester on an early computer model to determine "The Limits to Growth," a role that impacted his work and dedication to environmental issues.

In 1969, I planned a three-week vacation to Europe and returned to the U.S. six years later. During this time, I studied German and later Spanish, living, working, and studying in Germany and Spain. I studied English Philology at the University at Frankfurt. In 1974, I married a Valencian, Luis Valls-Verdejo, and we moved to Boston. Our marriage did not last, although our friendship did. In 1975, I began work at MIT. I met Michael at MIT in the spring of 1977 working on a project together. We were married in 1978 and moved to New Jersey. All this time, I continued my studies for a bachelor's degree. In 1979, after fourteen years, I received a B.A. in Modern Languages from a university without walls, Thomas Edison College in New Jersey. Six months later, I finished my master's in education at Rutgers.

In 1980, Michael and I moved to Detroit, Michigan, where Jonathan was born in 1982. During our tenure there I completed my doctoral coursework and comprehensives in Adult & Continuing Education. In 1985, we moved to Zionsville, Pennsylvania (a great farm), where I wrote my dissertation, completing my studies in 1990.

My work life reflects an ability to adapt to whatever is needed wherever I am located. While in Europe, I worked in real estate development, as a language teacher, and at odd jobs typical of college students: tutor, trade fair representative, etc. After MIT, where I worked at the Whitaker Health Sciences Fund and later found work as a Coordinator/Counselor at a pilot program in New Jersey called the Displaced Homemakers Center. I maintain an active interest in the advancement of women and, later, in Pennsylvania, served the Lehigh County Commissioners as a Member and Chair of their Women's Advisory Board. After finishing my doctorate, I juggled parental responsibilities with a 3/4-time job as Executive Director of a community mediation service, Common Ground. I became a certified mediator and oversaw a court-referred program to mediate landlord/tenant disputes, family visitation disputes, and employer/employee mediations. I also trained in peer mediation faculty and students at a number of public elementary and secondary schools.

In 1992, El Paso, Texas, offered me new opportunities. I was asked by the president of Providence Memorial Hospital to found a medical residency program. Over three years of working with Texas Tech Medical School, we successfully launched five residency programs. At the same time, I worked with the hospital's international marketing program to provide continuing medical education to Mexican physicians and their staff at identified clinics in Mexico. This was a great adventure for all of us! Finally, I served as principal investigator for the first collaborative Community Health Needs Assessment in El Paso. The consortium included the county hospital, Beaumont — a military hospital — Providence, the not-for-profit hospital, higher education institutions, and local community service agencies. I found that to be interesting and rewarding.

We moved from El Paso to the Boston area in 1995. Jonathan was in eighth grade. I found it too difficult to pursue full-time work while trying to meet his transportation needs and provide emotional support. I didn't realize how isolated wealthy suburban children can be. I made the choice to dedicate that relatively short time in my life to supporting Jonathan in a critical developmental time in his life. I volunteered at the high school, attended a year-long Chinese course with him, and generally held down the fort during typical teenage years. It was time well spent. Wayland High School is one of the few classical high schools that remain today. Jonathan had a tremendous education.

Now, I work for the SUNY chancellor as one of two of his liaisons to campus presidential searches. Again, it challenges me to learn something new, which I find most rewarding. I am still on the upward learning curve, but having developed some mastery, I'm beginning to enjoy the search business. Looking toward the future, I hope to continue this type of work as a consultant.

So now you have a two-dimensional look at the lives of Michael Luck and family. Since Michael became a father so young, his children are somewhat older than your nieces and nephews. Small glimpses of Kevin's girls appear familiar in photos of what Holly looked like as a child, offering a little trait here and there. As we grow older, we find children and grandchildren tend to reflect characteristics of uncles, aunts, and grandparents. So, it is likely we might discover some shared characteristics.

We left messages for Patrick in Berkeley and, as Michael reported, happily connected with him a day or two ago. We excitedly anticipate a reunion with him during his time on the East Coast, presently scheduled for September. He is a wonderful man whom we greatly love and enjoy, and we would like to spend time with him again. Now I know where he is I can reactivate my "snail mail" correspondence with him!

Best wishes for a productive and rewarding summer!
Love from,
Barbara with Michael

Terry let me know that he was not wasting any time. Almost immediately, he called Pat and explained Donna's secret story about me. He mentioned that he and Idanna had already met Barbara and me, and they were quite enamored. Terry asked Pat if he would be agreeable to his sharing the news with his other brothers. Fortunately, he agreed such an announcement was long overdue. Next, Terry contacted his three brothers. He told each the story of Donna's deathbed wishes and that Pat wanted them to know.

Meanwhile, Barbara sent an e-mail to Jonathan, Holly, and Sean. It was Holly's birthday!

December 04, 2003
Dear Sean, Holly, and Jonathan,
Our spirits are revived after a phenomenal first meeting with Michael's half-brother, Terry Ward, and his wife, Idanna Pucci. They are intelligent, informed, and socio-politically compatible with an absolute passion for life and making a difference. Michael attended Terry's presentation at the UN yesterday (I was unable to go with work commitments). He presented to the "World Conference on Religion and Peace," the book he wrote about his family's experience going back to Iran, where they lived while Pat was employed by Aramco Oil Company. The journey was undertaken after decades of absence to find the man and his family that took care of them for all the time they were in Iran. The book was called Searching for Hassan. The book, plus Terry's expertise on Iran/Middle Eastern culture and history, made the presentation noteworthy. Michael said it was fabulous and filled with such humanitarian energy.

We think Idanna is a spirit who has been on earth at least three times before. Indeed, she is a centered and reflective person. She is a rare individual with a deep intellect who has survived the complete chaos of life as a Marquesa under the tutelage of a wild and sometimes crazy father incapable of true affection for his children. The personal story intertwines with the historical one, which spans 800 years of family history embodied in the Pucci Palace, located one block from the Duomo in the center of Florence. Idanna and Terry are environmental and social activists who put their money where their mouths are. They demonstrated against the G-8 in Genoa and spoke eloquently and gracefully in support of their ideals. Needless to say, it was a splendid evening.

As you know, our first meeting with Terry and Idanna was at the National Arts Club, a national historic landmark. It was a vaunted space replete with brilliant works of art and architecture. We met under the glass dome in the bar. On one side of the bar was a painting of suffragettes deep in conversation, while the other side was populated with a gaggle of artists, friends, and ladies wearing fashionable hats! Terry told a story about one of the ladies wearing an especially noteworthy hat. Terry said, "I think she lives in a three-room apartment — two of them house her hats!"

We soon left the bar and rambled through back corridors and up old elevators to Terry and Idanna's studio apartment. It has a lovely window looking out over Grammercy Park. What a place. On the way, we encountered the club's Executive Director, Alden James. Apparently, James has been a friend of the Ward family for a considerable time. We had just visited his bronze bust, created by none other than Terry's brother, Christopher Ward. The whole experience was surreal, openly engaging, and heart-warming.

Apparently, the next day, Terry called his father to say he met his fifth brother, Michael! Pat had no idea Donna had shared with Terry all the details about him before she died.

Now, a new chapter in all our lives is unfolding. We are reassured our lives will be further enriched by these new associations. What good fortune we have.

Love,
Dad and Mom (Barbara)

The meetings and all the correspondence made the message clear. Even though there was not a shared past, Pat now had five sons.

~ 18 ~

WARDIAN ACCEPTANCE

On December 15, Barbara and I were ecstatic to be introduced to two more Ward brothers, Christopher and Kevin, only ten days after our initial meeting with Terry and Idanna. Things were moving so quickly that I barely had time to process my emotions.

Once again, at the National Arts Club, we received warm hugs and kisses, and it felt wonderful. It was the holiday season, and the Ward clan often celebrated together in the city. Barbara and I met brother Chris, a sculptor who lives with his family in Philadelphia and was there visiting Pat, who had arrived from California for their family gathering. Chris was tall like me, handsome, and adroit at what he did. He, too, was blessed with the Irish blarney.

The Wards are a family of great storytellers, and many were unfolded with great zeal and determined humor. Some were stories of bravado, notably athletic adventures and events of family lore. Comfortably situated in Terry's NAC studio apartment, Patrick and Christopher were laughing and enjoying themselves when Kevin arrived, just in from the UK. It was a thrill to meet my third brother. He was there with his wife, Helen, to host their annual holiday party. The two had lived in NYC for years and accumulated many friends and associates.

Kevin broke out a robust smile that brightened the room. He opened his arms wide, not only embraced us heartily, but also graciously invited us to join in the Wardian falderol at Kevin's holiday reception. This appeared to be a good sign. It was as if I had passed the family litmus test.

I said, "We would be honored to accept your invitation." It was then it dawned on me that the holiday party was a great setting for my new brothers to introduce me to local family and friends. The stage was set, the script written, and the inclusive event would be replete with surprises! This was my debut! They were introducing a new family member, and I felt validated, included, and grateful.

The National Arts Club was lavishly decorated with holiday excess and elegance. It was breathtaking. With more than a little trepidation, Barbara and I ascended the familiar stairs to the salon. This festive evening would be a grand opening night for one and all.

Pat's brother, Sean (my new uncle), was there. He had spent the summer with Pat at the Edgewood Resort fifty-three years before and knew all the details of Rita and Pat's story. Sean's wife, Flo, was there with him as Barbara took her hand and gestured, "The man standing over there is my husband, Michael Luck. He is Pat Ward's fifth son."

Flo gave a knowing nod and said, "Pat and Sean had wonderful tales about their time in the Catskills."

Sean, resigned to a wheelchair and suffering from Alzheimer's, was particularly animated. Without prompting, he did remember his time at the resort from a half-century ago. He talked about the events and fateful decisions made with his brother, Pat. He exclaimed with some theatrical emphasis and halting speech, "So, Michael, you're Pat's big secret? I'm glad it all turned out for the best. You look like a grand Irish lad with an appropriate Wardian mustache." The moment was poignant.

Quickly, the news of my presence made its way around the crowded salon like a game of telephone tag. The evening was a blur of faces, names, and family genealogy. I had to remind myself it would take a while to get to know one another better. All in good time. There was no rush. I was mindful to be in the moment and take it all in. After all, I was meeting many family members for the first time!

Barbara and I departed, dizzy with the excitement of the evening and grateful to be included in the event. We bid farewell to what felt like new friends and family. It was a joyously sad moment. The promise of other gatherings lessened the heartache.

We went back to our hotel room and stayed up late, talking about everyone we had met after years of searching. We laughed about some of the stories and admittedly tall tales shared by various family raconteurs that made the Irish Ward clan seem bigger than life.

Later, we arranged visits with each of the brothers. The first trip was to see Chris and his family at their home in Philadelphia. Then, on to London to see Kevin's family and then the one brother not yet embraced, Richard and his family in Leiden, Netherlands.

As promised, we kept in touch through letters and phone calls. I brimmed with emotion each time.

I quickly crafted a note to Terry.

Dear Terry and Idanna,
Look what you have unleashed!
You are a prince and a princess!! Thank you so much for the warmth of sentiment and thoughtfulness. Your kind words are a source of pleasure and inspiration. I am so full of excitement and so proud of you and all my brothers. Pat called last night and talked with Barbara and then put Kevin on so we could chat for a while. It was the only other occasion since the wonderful Ward soiree at the National Arts Club that we have had the chance to speak to each other.
I promised Kevin when we complete our plan to visit Rich in early spring, we shall stop in London to see him as well. I also suggested our home in the mountains of Vermont was always available to enjoy country life. I will call Kevin early on Christmas Eve to talk with Pat. We plan to see him while he is in Berkeley this winter.

I mentioned to Pat that Barbara and I would love to become members of the National Arts Club. We have rarely been any place where we both felt so comfortable and so much at home. Whatever applications, references, or fees are needed I would be thrilled to supply them. Just let me know how to proceed.

In the year ahead, I hope you will alert us when your schedule brings you into reasonable proximity. We adore you both and hope to see you when you sign another "big book" deal in New York City. Clearly, I would be honored to host you for champagne at the Arts Club in celebration. In the meantime, please accept our giant hugs and kisses for the holidays and the year ahead.

May the love from our house keep you safe and sound until we have a chance to meet again. You have reminded me of my favorite quote from Horace Mann: "Be ashamed to die until you have won some victory for humanity."

You are King Pat's "global knights," and I love you both.
Big hugs and lots of love,
Michael and Barbara

Terry wrote back.

Bless you, Michael, for all the unfolding layers over the last several weeks. Astounding... poignant and an emotional odyssey from the heart. I can't tell you what a thrill it is to see you are corresponding with Chris, acting as an older brother for him. Also, to read how you and Pat spoke tenderly about his/our loss of Donna, but at the same time, had the sagacity as his son to remind him of the need to celebrate her memory with laughter.

Dad always taught us life is indeed theater. With tragedy, of course, there is always comedy. This profound mystery is all-consuming and revealing for us mortals. It has always been thus. So, when the lights go up at your home before Christmas, please give your/our Barbara a warm embrace from Idanna and me. Tell Jonathan that his uncle and aunt are proud of him and his bold, less-traveled path.

Give a kiss to your other children, their partners, and kiddies from afar, and tell them we will meet soon. Above all, on a cold winter night before Christmas, step outside and look into the far heavens dancing in their eternal passage and remember seven hundred years ago, Hafez was thinking of you, when he wrote: "Let us be crowned with roses and let us drink wine, and tonight, we shall break up the tiresome roof of heaven into new forms."

In the moment, with your Barbara, listen to the heavens roar, my brother!

Love supreme,
Terry with Idanna

***

Our first visit was to see Chris, Julia, and family in Philadelphia, Pennsylvania. They lived in a nineteenth-century historic Chestnut Hill home, which originally belonged to Julia's parents. All three generations resided in the beautiful home, each caring for one another. Time with Chris and Julia's sons, Laurenson and Dylan, was a special treat.

Chris immediately shared with me his tale of how he discovered he had another brother.

He said, "I clearly remember the day Terry called and announced, 'I have some great news, Cooch (Chris's nickname). Are you sitting down? We have another brother... a brother from another mother."

Chris then admitted he gushed, "What? How is this great news?"

He then asked Terry, "Does Dad know?"

Terry responded, "Of course, he's known for quite a long time!"

Chris retorted, "How about Kev? So then, is Michael the oldest?"

Terry said, "Yes, Michael's the oldest."

Chris said he thought hard about the new information. Philosophical and practical arguments about "nature versus nurture" flashed through his head. He said he wondered "Would I look like his father?" "Would I be like his other brothers?" Chris knew all the Ward family members were outsized characters ready for the stage or screen. The only fear at any family gathering was silence and any topic was a toss-up.

Chris then leaned over and whispered to me, "Despite all my early reservations, all my questions were answered when I first met you a while ago at the National Arts Club. It was your beaming smile and bear hug greeting which suggested you were a Ward on the paternal side."

After a house tour, Chris invited us to his art studio on the lower floor of the house. Bronze sculpture was the love of his life and his core talent. Similar to other artists, he engaged in other less artistic employment to provide a steady income for his family. With his extraordinary talent, his bronze sculpture commissions brought him great satisfaction and recognition.

Chris commented, "What a gift life is...the mysteries and abundance of wonderful possibilities."

In 2004, Barbara and I flew into the sunrise of new beginnings. First, visiting with Rich, his wife Ellen, and their two sons, Brendan and Ames, in Leiden, the Netherlands. He was the only brother we hadn't met. Rich and El's home was filled with emotional warmth as the greeting came, "Hello, brother!! This is such a wonderful occasion. Even though I'm the last brother to meet you, I'm not the least! I'm thrilled you've come to see us. You are so tall, and you look just like all your photos. How was the trip? Did El find you okay at the airport? We have plenty of time to talk while we dine and have boat tours and bike rides. We want you to see us as well as Leiden's canals and arched bridges."

Rich and El's home, a beautiful historic multi-storied apartment, included a top floor just for play. It was festooned with ropes suspended like a spider's web across the ceiling. It was an optimal place for fantasy, imagination, and mood. Maybe it was my hard-wired taste, but I loved the house with such an array of unique cultural artifacts collected from El's artist mother and their eleven-year life in Saudi Arabia. Rich was especially engaged with Middle

Eastern artifacts and style. It was as much an ethnic cultural center as a home.

During dinner, El proposed the agenda for the next day. It included a guided tour of Leiden's canals by "Captain Rich" on a private barge boat followed by a bike excursion to see city highlights. There was a comfortable ease of conversation. I was mesmerized by Rich's description of his current aesthetic experiment: the production of cardboard collapsible animal masks. The masks were flat like origami for storage and quickly transformed into a 3D authentic animal face. My mind swirled with how such clever costume faces could be marketed for Halloween or upscale favors for child and adult festivities. It was a natural creative connection.

A knock at the door brought Rich and El's two sons from school. Ames and Brendan, taller than their parents, were a perfect blend of both. The two nephews were curious to meet us, their new "Uncle" Michael and "Aunt" Barbara. Questions flowed: "How do you like Leiden? How is school? How is it different from where you used to be? Have you made friends? Are you happy?"

The dialogue continued for hours. Both boys were delighted they had someone to listen to all their stories, a natural family proclivity. The visit built a brotherly bond. All too soon, there were kisses, hugs, and promises to see each other again, and we were off to London to see Kevin and his family.

***

Once settled in a boutique hotel near Hampstead Heath, we called Kevin to announce our arrival. He was expecting the call and provided short walking directions to his home.

As we strolled up the street to Kevin's home, he and his daughter, Kyra, suddenly appeared walking toward us. Our first meeting with seven-year-old Kyra was a delight. She was fascinated with this new man whom her father called a brother. She knew she had three uncles, but now she had four. The ten-minute stroll provided enough time to get reacquainted and talk with Kyra about school. My other niece, Catherine, was waiting at home.

After arriving at Kevin's home, we talked for hours. Kevin, currently working as an independent entrepreneur, had a corporate subscription business plan that involved creating virtual customized human resource computer training videos. Arriving a few hours later, Helen arrived from a week of work on the road. She traveled most weeks for a large public relations and marketing firm. Her principal clients were in California, so her travel was tedious, and she was absent for large blocks of time. She enjoyed her job, but the demands of her family were demonstrable. As Kevin and Helen prepared an evening dinner, she spoke about her work as well as plans for all of us the next day in nearby Hampstead Heath.

After morning coffee, the next day, Barbara and I were launched into high-speed games with Kyra and Catherine on the meadows of Hampstead Heath. Both girls had remarkable energy, a precocious style, and natural beauty. The first game was a playful soccer match. Barbara, the designated goalie, made unbelievable saves, much to the surprise and chagrin of the two nieces. The day was filled with a reflective atmosphere woven together with two high-energy girls engaged in an age-appropriate "attention at all costs" performance.

I cleaned up the red wine that Kyra had spilled on the carpet while Catherine accidentally broke one of the cabinets. Moments later, while we were all preoccupied with conversation, Kyra enthusiastically ate all the irresistible dessert strawberries by dipping them into a bowl of cream and then a dish of brown sugar. It was no wonder Helen and Kevin were exhausted. It was clear when the two girls' mother was home that the family dynamic devolved into a spirited ballet of keeping two young divas out of mischief. I thought everyone was marvelous and captivating and enjoyed every minute.

Oh, to be young again!

~ 19 ~

THE RUDDERLESS SHIP

Understandably, Donna's death was a devasting loss for the family loss, especially for Pat. Although Barbara and I were unable to attend Donna's memorial service, we did arrange a subsequent visit to see Pat. He was alone. After spending time with each of his sons, he needed to adjust to life by himself. As Donna had been an irreplaceable rudder in Pat's life, he now had to steer his own ship and recalibrate his bearings to make sense of his new reality.

When Pat returned to his Spruce Street home, he settled into familiar surroundings with Donna still missing. Most days, Pat's custom was to jump in his car, release the brake, and let it coast down Spruce Street at high speed until he reached the stop sign at Marin. Then, he'd turn to go straight to the gym, where he, at least symbolically, hinted at physical exertion. Mostly, he shared his brilliance for telling stories with other older men like himself, who shared some of his contrarian views. Most days, Pat's gym visit involved just enough time to count as a satisfactory workout, even though he had barely ever changed his clothes. On his way home, if he felt especially effervescent, he would pick up a couple of Nathan's hot dogs with the works (his favorites) and drive home. Then, he would sit with a good book and, perhaps, dent a bottle of wine.

***

We arrived at Pat's for a planned visit for a few nights in the fall of 2004 and were fondly welcomed. Our time together provided a great outlet for one of Pat's passions, theatre. It was one of my passions, too. As Pat purchased tickets for an evening performance, we learned we were his first official guests since Donna's death. It was evident Pat still missed the comfort of his old habits and social tics. The rhythm in the house was somewhat new and different, perhaps even a little off-kilter. Pat sometimes grumbled he was too old to start a new life.

I was thrilled to spend time with my father. It was easier to communicate when others weren't wrestling for attention. Barbara was helpful in preparing small meals in the kitchen. Pat would eat practically anything. Over coffee, much could be discussed in a quiet and honest manner. There were moments when Pat was guarded and others when he was glib and entertaining. He had depended on Donna to be his social foil, manager, and relationship guardian. Now, he had to fend for himself and recreate all the social scripts. It would take some practice.

A great pleasure for Pat was showing me the backyard fruit trees he claimed to tend every day. Upon surveying the small orchard, I suspected that he just looked at them most days. The trees were sprinkled across the steep slope behind the house, where a winding path connected them all from top to bottom. I discovered traveling down the path was easy, it was the return uphill that was slow. The yard was eclectic and, at the same time, attractive. It had a variety of trees, flowering plants, and bushes designed to create an appealing retreat with minimal maintenance. Walking together provided a calming respite for both of us.

I shared with Pat that I had successfully applied for Irish citizenship under the country's Descendancy Program. It granted anyone with grandparents born and married in Ireland the opportunity to become a citizen. I smiled happily as I shared with Pat that on July 1, 2004, a FedEx envelope had arrived at my home. Inside was an official certificate of Irish citizenship. It made me feel close to him, like belonging to an authentic family tree. In a low voice, I leaned over to Pat to say, "I held the citizenship papers in my hands a long time and stared at the mix of Gaelic and English words and signatures. It was a proud and defining moment for me. Thank you."

My Irish passport came later. Pat said, "You must use your new passport to make your first trip to Ireland. When you pass through the passport control, they will say, 'Welcome home!!' With Barbara's Irish background and yours, you will both enjoy the adventure. There are Wards still there, still living in the old homestead."

Then he added, "Have you seen a white envelope lying around? It contains the tickets for tonight's play."

Pat shared a few comments about his memory problems and inability to keep close track of items around the house. He had scoured all the usual haunts: his pants pockets, jacket pockets, and the key tray. I told him that my adoptive father, Bill, experienced similar lapses in memory and not to worry. We would help him find the tickets. We did.

At one point, Pat looked at me with weepy blue eyes and said, "I have to tell you a heartfelt story from long ago, about the first time I took Rita to my mother and father's house in Bayonne. While there, I regaled her with our Ward family story of the 'Magical Christmas Tree.'" I told Rita I believed in Santa Claus until I was nine years old. This belief was not because of naiveté but because of my mother. She came from County Donegal in Ireland, a place where leprechauns are born and thrive. Most believe such little creatures really do exist. This leprechaun belief caused me to incorporate a profound mystic and childlike imagination reinforced by my mother. Once reinforced, the idea of Santa Claus was an easy and natural extension."

He continued, "Weeks before Christmas the excitement in our house was palpable. Everyone frenetically joined in holiday activities and wrote hopeful messages to Santa. These messages were carefully written by my mother as dictated by each child. Every Santa letter started the same way, with warm banter about the reindeer, thanking Santa for past visits to our house, and expressing warm appreciation for any previous gifts received. I was always thanking Santa for a pair of socks, underwear, occasional sweaters, and maybe a toy. Once, Santa gave me a genuine Indian costume complete with a headdress. The outfit consisted of a pair of old play pants with fringe sewn on and a band of feathers, which smelled fresh. Knowing my mother, they had been recently plucked from the family chicken to be eaten on Christmas Day. All our family Christmas's thrilled me to no end.

Aside from the long Santa letters, there were other important Christmas preparations. My mother always reminded us to put any stale bread on the back porch to feed the reindeer. Then, after dinner on Christmas Eve, we were all promptly sent to bed, trembling with anticipation but without a decorated tree. She then quickly busied herself, making a pot of tea and preparing a slice of pound cake to share with Santa as a snack.

Our mother always claimed Santa brought our Christmas tree and helped her decorate it. So, every Christmas morning, we awoke to find a fully decorated tree aglow with lights. It was only years later that I discovered my mother's real stratagem was to get a tree for free by waiting until Christmas Eve when many unbought trees were left over, and a kind-hearted tree salesman might make a gift. The worst-case scenario was she had to buy one, but it would at least, be cheap. Our mother calculated a Christmas Eve buyer was in the driver's seat for negotiations, so the discounts were steep.

The plan worked flawlessly for years until my mother woke me at midnight on one fateful Christmas Eve because I was the oldest. She asked me to come to the kitchen. There was a sad look on her face as she described the circumstances, 'Pat, I have to tell you something you won't want to hear: there is no Santa Claus. I know how crushed you may be to hear this news, but now I need your help. Santa never brought a tree to our house; I did. Tonight, I have been all over town trying to find one, and there is none to be had.

So, you and I have to make one. God help us! How the wee ones will be disappointed without a tree when they wake up.'

"My mother had gathered a pile of pine branches from a sympathetic tree salesman. She swiftly got the kitchen broom, stuck the 'sweeping end' into a bucket, and asked me to get wire, braids, and string from the kitchen drawer. With careful precision, the two of us attached the pine branches to the broomstick. After enough branches were attached, lights, some colorful decorations, and a final overload of silver tinsel were added. The tinsel judiciously hid a multitude of obvious imperfections, so I added more. Then Mom asked me to plug in the tree lights and said, 'Patrick, isn't it the most beautiful sight you've ever seen?'

"I had to agree. However, there was no time to waste. There were presents to put under the tree and other Santa tricks to unveil. To convince the children that Santa came down the chimney, Mother scattered stove ashes on the kitchen floor and around the tree. She felt there was no sense in overdoing it as the ashes on the living room floor were harder to clean up.

"Mother then said, 'Oh, I almost forgot, Patrick, go get the stale bread your brothers scattered on the back porch for the reindeer.'

"Surprised, I exclaimed, 'Why?'

"Mother replied, 'God help you, sweetie, we never throw the bread out. I need it to make Christmas stuffing for us to eat tomorrow. Then, Mother said, 'Let's have a cup of tea and a slice of pound cake I made for Santa. Then, you need to go off to bed with a kiss.'

"To this day, I still think spending Christmas Eve helping my mother might have been my best ever. Christmas morning, there were shrieks of delight and surprise as our mother dramatized the details of Santa's visit a few short hours before. Santa had brought in the tree, helped decorate it, accidentally left ashes on the floor from his boots, the reindeer had eaten all the bread, and Santa had enjoyed his cup of tea and pound cake.

"My mother then winked and looked at all of us and said, 'Santa had told me what wonderful children I had.'

"Absentmindedly, my mother almost blew it when she asked my brother, 'James, go to the closet and get the broom so I can sweep up Santa's ashes.'

"James reported, 'Mother, the broom isn't there!'

"Miraculously, without missing a beat, Mother said, 'Well, what do you know, Santa was complaining about dust on his sled, and I loaned him my broom; it will probably be another year before we get it back, so I'll have to go and buy another one.'

"None of us ever saw the tree come down as we were all off to school at the time, and my brothers wouldn't even notice the broom suddenly reappear. My mother made me promise not to tell anyone or ever breathe a word about being Santa's helper. I never did.

"Many years later, when visiting with my brothers and sisters, we were reminiscing about Christmases that had long passed. We talked about the excitement of Christmas mornings, and we all agreed we had the prettiest tree, except one year when they all remembered it looked a bit scruffy. Of course, I thought it was the best time we ever had because I helped Momma create the 'Magic Christmas Tree' for her wee ones. I didn't tell them the truth."

Pat's blue eyes were misty as he whispered, "It's a great story, isn't it?"

Barbara and I sat transfixed with tears in our eyes, too. Pat's story was endearingly personal and poignant. In some ways, it wasn't the story as much as the way Pat told it. His eyes twinkled, and his entire face lit up as he revealed each piece of the tale. Every word seemed to make him feel near his mother and helped me feel closer to him.

Pat then exclaimed that he had carried the Magic Christmas Tree tradition to Iran when his first son, Kevin, arrived as a "wee one" and that the other three were born. The four boys would wake up to brand-new presents Santa brought from America. He chuckled,

"I still think all my boys believed in Santa till they went off to high school, or at least, they pretended to do so for my benefit!"

In a grand Irish tradition, Pat told his boys there's a whole world of magic in life, just around the corner and behind every tree. The unimaginative could never see the magic because they didn't believe it and didn't pay enough attention. But, if attentive, an "ordinary world" turned into a "magical" one in a flash. If you look hard enough, magical adventures reveal themselves and beg you to come along. He claimed the Irish believe that magic adds color and a sense of potential to everyone's already full lives; anything's possible.

With a twinkle, Pat said, "Now, do you want to hear about some of my military exploits? Both amused, Barbara and I were thrilled with his attention. Clearly, Pat was on a roll and was happy to share his memories. He held our attention with his amazing feat as the boxing phenom called "The Dancing Master," his exploits as a bombardier in a WWII B-17, and his exploits with Aramco in Iran on how he convinced camel caravans not to destroy the oil pumping power stations.

~ 20 ~

CHEATED BY DEATH

The Ward family rallied around Pat. Each did their part to help fill the irreplaceable void in his life. The strategy was to keep him engaged with family and friends as part of the recovery process. Everyone in the family kept abreast of his exploits.

Terry had suggested Pat come and stay in Florence and he would take him on a trip to Iran to revisit old haunts as well as Hassan and his family. He hoped the spiritual journey might renew his father's zest for life. He was certain an emotional homecoming would await them in Isfahan, with warm embraces from old dear friends.

Pat responded, "I'm ready to go, Ter; let's do it!"

The plan was for Pat to fly from California to New York, stay a few days, adjust to the three-hour time change, and then proceed to Florence. While in New York City, he'd stay in Terry's apartment at the NAC and see family and old friends, including a special trip to the racetrack with his nephew Kurt. Several days later, Terry would greet him in Florence before their last journey to Iran. A plan was made to deliver donated handicap equipment to children and adults wounded in the Iran/Iraq war. The mission for Pat was to return to Iran with a shared common purpose to help others, that he so deeply shared with Donna. It was all just what he needed.

***

Upon arrival at the NAC, Pat happily greeted longtime friends and settled comfortably into Terry's apartment. He strolled around the neighborhood to greet old friends and acquaintances he had not seen since Donna's passing.

Along the way, he stopped in to see his old Greek buddy, Petros, who owned Pete's Diner on Third Avenue and 21st Street. There were big hugs and warm greetings. Apparently, Petros vociferously complained about the political criminals in Washington, D.C. Pat put his arm around his shoulder, looked him in the eye, and said, "Petros, life's too short. Take a deep breath and look at the bright side."

Petros reached below the counter and pulled out a bottle of his prized Santorini wine. "You're right, Pat. Let's have a toast!"

Filling two glasses, he beamed with a loud "Yassou!" as the two pals grandly toasted each other with roaring laughter. Pat was fully energized and happy to be back in familiar territory.

When Pat returned to Terry's flat, he called Kurt to confirm plans for the next day to have fun betting on the horses at the racetrack. He was looking forward to his time with Kurt and jovially expressed his delight at being back in New York,

He said to Kurt, "They're treating me like returning royalty, red carpet and all! See you tomorrow."

When Pat did not appear at the appointed time to depart for the racetrack, the family began to worry. Although it wasn't entirely unusual for Pat to devise his own plan, take a nap, or even get lost, this was out of character. Certainly, Pat would arrive soon. Kurt was unsettled. To arrive as scheduled, he had to leave by three p.m. Pat was not there. There were unsuccessful phone calls to Pat's cell phone and the NAC, and they exclaimed, "Yes, we've seen him. He must be out and about." Then, the NAC staff even knocked on Terry's apartment door, but no one answered.

Concern darkened with thoughts Pat must have been injured, confused, or even had forgotten about the event. Seriously concerned, Kurt asked if the NAC staff could unlock Terry's apartment and enter to be sure everything was okay. The NAC staff knocked on the door, called Pat's name, and unlocked the door to enter.

To their great dismay, they found Pat lying on the kitchen floor, semiconscious. They rushed to his side to help him. He was alive, barely coherent, and couldn't speak. Some guessed he could have been lying there for some time. Soon, the EMTs whisked him away to Cabrini Medical Center. It seemed Pat may have lost his balance and fallen onto the kitchen floor from the stairs or simply collapsed, striking his head. No one knew for sure. The impact caused a significant head injury. At Pat's age, his medical diagnosis was poor. There had been significant hemorrhaging, which, left untreated, had only exacerbated the problem.

Chris was the first son to rush to his side at the Cabrini Hospital, followed later by all the brothers. In and out of consciousness, occasionally Pat opened his eyes and responded to verbal cues or a squeeze of his hand. He appeared to understand what was being said. A brain scan provided tragic news. In addition to the serious brain injury, Pat also had some sort of brain cancer. A second brain scan confirmed the diagnosis. The medical team informed the family that the hemorrhaging was deep and it wasn't all caused by his fall.

Rich received the telephone message about his father while pacing in the hallway of his home. Eventually, he lay down tragically fatigued. His legs were shaking, and he was unable to support him any longer. Rich began to focus on life without his father. He said so to his wife Ellen, "El, it's just the sense of time. Dad, with all his poetry and drama, may well see his own death as a demonstration of his love for Donna. He stayed on the floor after his fall so he could just fade into heaven."

Rich's son, Ames, had tears running down his face when he learned of the possibility of life without his grandfather. "Grandpa can't die before he buries Grandma's ashes! Even though he once almost accidentally broke my arm, I'm still willing to try to make him happy by pushing his wheelchair around so he can play croquet with me."

It was left to Rich to call Kevin and give him all the details with admonishment: "Hey, Kev, Dad's not doing well. We need you. Please come! This is a time when we all need to be at the hospital for him."

I learned of Pat's tragic condition from Terry. I made plans to join the others, accompanied by Barbara and Jonathan. We drove to the city and the hospital, making it as quickly as possible. Some brothers were already assembled, anxiously hovering outside Pat's room for any news. We went to Pat's bedside to offer hugs and expressions of love and gratitude. With a squeeze of his hand, Pat seemed to recognize that we were there. It was a heartbreaking moment for all. We stayed outside his room, respecting the devastation and grief of everyone there.

Each of my brothers responded to Pat's predicament in a different manner: Chris (Cooch) offered him warm, tender caresses with intense logical analysis, while Kevin repeated his favorite reference for Pat as "Daddio," so he might recognize the deeply held feelings. At the same time, Terry was outwardly demonstrative, trying to connect with the embrace of shared love, while Rich offered a knowing balance with steady, responsive caring.

Aside from that, I made some time to consult with the Cabrini medical authorities about Pat's condition. With my work in healthcare, I knew doctors and nurses tend to be optimistic and hopeful in their pronouncements. They're rarely inclined to make negative statements. As I suspected, the medical reports were not encouraging.

We all experienced disbelief, helplessness, and a need to do something. Should he stay at Cabrini Hospital, or is there a better place nearby that could help him? What if he improved adequately and was transferred to rehabilitation? Where might he go? Philadelphia with Chris was the best and easiest choice. He was the closest to NYC. Constructive, although difficult, plans were explored for Pat's long-term care. We also offered to assist in the process, with Pat moving closer to us in Albany. It was a desperate attempt by all of us to change the subject to his survival and not face the foreboding outcome.

Sadly, the prospect of Pat dying after the loss of Donna a year earlier was undeniable. In his final hours, I sensed it was time to hold Pat's hand and extend love, respect, and dignity to a wonderful man and my father.

By the following day, there was a perceptible shift in mood from "Let's Save Pat" to the painful, inevitable acceptance that it was hopeless. We spent some time by Pat's bedside. There was a need to say goodbye. With pooling tears, Barbara moved to sit by Pat, holding his hand gently and telling him how grateful she was for his gift of Michael and her son Jonathan. Pat was a gift to all of us. Her eyes filled with tears when she received Pat's gentle hand squeeze of affirmation. Jonathan also shared his thoughts and feelings with his grandfather, second only to Grandpa Luck. Then, I held Pat's hand in a sorrowful moment to express my gratitude for his recognition of me as his son, making possible my three children, Sean, Holly, and Jonathan, and remorse that our time together was way too short. Such goodbyes always take a person's breath away. Forevermore, a parting moment in the Irish song, 'The Parting Glass.'

My four brothers remained with their father. Each came to the moment of separation with the weightiness of unconditional love. Rich said he wanted to remain by Pat's side since he had been uncertain about his mother's care near the end of her life. Terry struggled to craft adequate words to reflect his deep sorrow to his beloved father. Chris prayed for his father's soul to be received honorably in heaven. Kevin, overwhelmed, despite his natural eloquence for words, relied on quiet motion to soothe his father. This was a new beginning for family storytelling, Pat's tales indelibly etched with new importance and meaning.

As Pat passed away, the morning's sunshine lifted high to celebrate his eternal reunion with Donna. After the inevitable shock of loss, grief settled over everyone. Fatigued by travel, lack of sleep, and the devastation of Pat's passing, the morning revealed that the best way to celebrate Pat's life should be at the NAC, the home of many happy and warm family memories. All who could come would find open arms among family scattered throughout the city and beyond. The club staff and local friends made arrangements for a memorial service several days later.

Irish tradition suggests in times of sorrow, there is an embrace from the community of family and friends. In Ireland, memorial services often include enough food and spirits to share to cover several days of weeping, laughing, and remembrance of those who have passed. At times, even strangers were included, more particularly if they had a bottle of Irish Whiskey under their arm. During Pat's service, the trick would be to limit the amount of storytelling. Although the stories were moving, they inspired others to reach for just one more, another tearful or hilarious tale to share, real or imagined.

Pat's life celebration was to be a classic Irish wake with a hefty bottle of Jamison's with shot glasses on a simple table next to a photo of Pat. This was the spot where anyone could stand and speak. All were invited to share memories of love and friendship sweeping over eighty years. Barbara, Jonathan and my son, Sean arrived from Massachusetts to join in the sorrowful moment of tears and laughter. Sean never had a chance to meet his grandfather.

As was tradition, Kevin valiantly stepped forward to open the gathering, briefly summarizing the Irish tradition of rising to speak. Eloquent as always, but saddened deeply by the moment, he bore witness to all gathered. He offered gratitude to all for joining in the poignant moment of celebration. Christopher, in spite of being visibly drained by the darkness and desperation of the previous days, rose to the occasion, brightened and gracefully spoke about parts of the long family legacy.

Terry and Rich took their turns, each speaking profoundly from their hearts. Terry wrote a moving poem, and Rich stepped forward to share family moments that inspired him. Each set the stage for a staggeringly sentimental and often hilarious reflection on Pat's life. Some contemporaries told stories of bravado and delusion when Pat was a young baseball player in the neighborhood. Those gathered gasped for air, laughing heartily about descriptions of the endless and harmless Wardian escapades. The room's temperature rose as story after story soared, leaving all knowing how much Pat and Donna would have reveled in that moment. It was a fine way to renew the body and soul from the deep sorrow of loss.

My heart pounded with a "drained-of-all-life" feeling as I took my turn to speak and reflect on a father I barely knew: "Reflecting on Pat's hospitalization and tragic death, my inclination was to recite Auden's 'Funeral Blues'; you know the one which ends with 'The stars are not wanted now, put everyone out. Pack up the moon and dismantle the sun, pour away the ocean, and sweep up the wood. For nothing now can ever come to any good,' but I resisted.

"Instead, I thought of Pat as Odysseus. He was an idealist and epic romantic, not unlike Odysseus...inspired to go out along routes 'full of turnings,' wanderings, and dangers — always to come home again — because there, life mattered most!

"At home, he played, slept, restored, and planned his work — all the while joining with Chris, Terry, Kevin, Rich, and his beloved wife, Donna, in a special circle of love. We can only imagine Pat reading to his grandchildren Edmond Spencer's *Fairy Queen* about St. George and the Dragon — saying, 'a dreadful enemy awaits — a foul friend, a dragon, dangerous and frightful to behold...'

"Pat, of course, would act out all the parts, encouraging those listening to dream with him because he was dreaming too. By doing so, he taught them all to believe in themselves, be resourceful and resilient, and carry on the good fight.

"We can imagine Pat teaching his grandchildren baseball, saying — 'Concentrate your forces — focus — keep your eye on the ball.' It's just like anything else in life: 'When you take a cut at the ball — swing with all of your might. Remember every swing is a second chance. Learn from the mistakes you made last time and one day – you'll hit the ball out of the park.'

"Pat was always on one more journey which would bring — at least some small measure of enlightenment into a darkening world.

"So, I join my brothers and all of you assembled here to behold Pat and Donna 'dancing together on the Milky Way."

With no loss for words and a stream of accolades for Pat, the service was as fine a tribute as I could remember. Everyone was eloquent, generous, and kind, emboldened by the familiarity of the people assembled. We were brave and soulful at the moment, and I was glad to share it with my brothers, their families, the extended Ward clan, and old friends. It was a fitting celebration of a remarkable life well lived. I felt I had done my best to pay homage to my birth father, although I hoped I'd find something at the memorial service to save me from feeling cheated of more time. I didn't.

***

As the event drew to a close, a hum of voices rejoiced in an original piece of music, written and played on the piano by Chris's son, Laurenson, as a tribute to his grandfather. Perhaps the music was a metaphor for Pat's remarkable lifetime performance as well as a glimpse at the stirring generations to come.

Pat had elevated all our spirits with a life well lived, and now it was our turn.

~ 21 ~

THE MAN IN THE WIND

My brothers agreed to follow Irish tradition; the oldest has to bury the father. I was given the honor of carrying a small box of Pat's ashes back to Ireland to distribute aside the family cottage and cemetery, where generations of Wards and all others lay.

It was the fall of 2005 when I wrote to Aunt Susie Ward Boyle. She lived in the historic Ward family cottage dating to the 1860's, located in a small fishing village Burtonport, Donegal, Ireland. It was the home for all the Ward family members leaving to make their way to America. In my letter I asked Aunt Susie if Barbara and I might come to Burtonport to meet her and spread Pat's ashes.

Aunt Susie replied.

March 17, 2005
Dear Michael and family,
It was great to get your letter, and you will never believe how many relations you have. We look forward to your visit. You have a busy life and have achieved a lot. It is quite different from our simple life here.

I married John, my childhood sweetheart. We were married for fifty years. John passed away three months before our Golden Anniversary. I still miss him. We lived in London and had five in our family: two girls and three boys. After John's death, I returned to my humble roots. I gave up my lovely home in London, but I am happy back here. I have family who visit often, and I go to them, too.

So, today being St. Patrick's Day, I thought I must write. You will find Ireland somewhat different to the life you have. However, I am sure you'll like the sentiment and sadness of all who left their homes in search of a better life. Some never returned. There's so much to tell you. I miss my cousins Pat and Donna and Jimmy Ward. We've kept in touch and bonded so well when they came to Ireland some years ago. Now Nancy Titus, Jimmy's daughter, is our link with family out there.

So, for now, I will finish. I will wait to hear next about your arrangements and when you will make your journey to Ireland. Regards to all the family.

Best wishes,
Susie Ward Boyle

Flying to Ireland is easy, but driving there requires dexterity. Everyone drives, more or less, on the left side of the road. Full concentration is required to stay in correct road lanes. This was difficult because the landscape was, at once, original and sweeping. The green hills provoked awe and fondness. I thought the idea of Ireland's emerald green was likely exaggerated, promulgated by people with big imaginations who'd never been there before, now I knew they were right.

Aunt Anne Marie (Pat's only living sister) and her husband, Karl Nygren, joined us for the family reunions and ceremony. The arrival at Susie's cottage was grand. Catching sight of the family homestead was breathtaking. One could almost hear voices rise to greet us. Susie flew out of the house with a smile and lilting cheer that would lighten up any dreary day. She had high Irish cheekbones with wide-set, sharp blue eyes, and a wondrous beaming face.

There, we were invited to share warm embraces and Irish hospitality with tea by the fire. Tea in Ireland isn't just tea, it's an occasion. It was time for Susie to tell the surest things she knew.

Her Donegal Irish lilt seemed to make all her sentences end with a question or an exclamation point.

I remembered Pat's brother, Jimmy's words:

At the old homestead there is a small lake below Lough Haraha and the nearby wild sea and far-off valleys. There, images of time past, with a white sun-washed cottage and yellow-thatched roof, almost become reality. The home door opens with a turf fire gleaming inside. Soft-strung violins hang on the wall as a reminder of the strong and happy men who once played them. Flash, the dog sits on a rug, cozy and clean, in front of the fire. As the kettle steams, an Irish woman stands ramrod straight with an apron and a beaming face, hoping to capture anyone coming for a visit.

Uncle Jimmy emphasized,

Ireland is magnificent as an epitome of Keats. All photos and literature cannot prepare a newcomer for its stunning haunting beauty. Donegal does not easily share its farmers or fishermen, all good at their trade without being boastful. Their good deeds shared only by others in tales. Even the pubs ring with laughter and grand gestures of treasured deeds from the past, as if repetition would turn them all into princes and playboys.

Lit by fireside, stories pass from one to another when the day's dusty duties are done. In a corner, stories were told about Neil and John Nelly when they gave away their feed of fish or Paddy Kitty's life was saved just off Lagichanty Rock as he was almost all done in. To celebrate the rescue, the family killed a fat hen, so there'd be soup with barley and potatoes, tea, scones, and hand-pitted currents.

The history of Gaelic storytellers belongs to antiquity, a time when there were no books, no radio, no cellphones, no cinema, or television. A time when the only entertainment may be a winter night's tale told by a passing traveler with "seanchaí," a special gift for telling tales of fairies, ghosts, and other supernatural beings. The stories could make time stand still.

It was easy to imagine old Mrs. Sharkey dressed in black with her arms outstretched, shawl flapping in the wind raging against the sea, praying for her husband, lost at sea. Or, if death came, ragged women in mourning "keening and raising doleful dolorosa" greater than the sea's own. The men might drink a shot or two of whiskey and accidentally let the sheep out of the bier or speak of the days when they were young and happy; the hay was in, they had a horse with daily chores of bringing in a creedal of turf for the fire or digging prates from the field.

Susie admonished us to remember to always smile first and say, "Good morning." She said, "A morning greeting is sometimes followed by a glance at a distant hill which cannot be found when walking toward it, but only when walking away. Up Corkscrew Hill, over a rise, past the bog fields, and beyond to the Atlantic, there's a spot where it's easy to imagine others traveled the same road and took to the sea. Irish emotions always run high. It's inborn, bountiful, and apparent.

Outside the old Ward homestead facing the Atlantic, near where wild roses grew and chickens pecked, I found a suitable place for some of Pat's ashes. It was a location where ancestors might have stood, searching the sky for a hint of favor. Pat was now home. He would be happy near Cloughglass, just past Dungloe and the Rosses, where no trees grow because of the steady wind and sandy soil. After the small ceremony, Aunt Susie suggested Pat would be happy. The Ward homestead was a place where one might hear that a grandfather clock was fifteen minutes slow, and the response would be, "Sure, it is. What's the difference? We're not going anyplace?"

In that magical moment, Aunt Susie loaded us into several cars to see an historic monument near the village. It was erected near an old rail station in 1968 as a testimonial and remembrance of James Duffy and my great Uncle, James Ward. The plaque read: "To commemorate the first action in the Tan War when the Irish volunteers rescued two comrades, James Duffy and James Ward, from British troops at this place on 4 January 1918." Aunt Susie was kind enough to regal us all with the important historical details.

Aunt Susie, as a first-class raconteur, reminded us that folks in Donegal have more stories to tell than anyone has the patience and time to hear. She said, for example, "In a countryside courtroom, a judge asked a young Irish lass a question. 'Was the suspect in the habit of singing alone?' "The Irish lass gushed, 'Well, I can't say for sure... I was never with him when he was alone.'"

By early the next morning, we gathered at the nearby Cruit cemetery to properly place the remainder of Pat's ashes. The cemetery held most of the extended Ward family members all in one place. With Susie Ward Boyle in the lead, under a sea of black umbrellas, the small entourage climbed a slight incline to a small plateau of headstones. The area of the Ward gravesite was on a spot of land rising above the quay. It was framed by a stone wall covered with vines like a living canvas. I measured the scale of names on the stones. Susie graciously described the relationship of each like an echo from a history book with the comment, "I'll be there soon enough!"

There were murmured explanations about the gravesite being in some disarray, getting crowded, and needing a bit of work. Aunt Anne Marie said she would send money to properly expand and beautify the entire section of the cemetery devoted to the Ward family so it was more suitable.

Back in the car, as we drove away, I quickly expressed the sentiment in my heart and wrote a simple homage on the back of a napkin.

On October 10, 2005:

A misty rain - a day of grey
Winding paths beside the quay
Cruit's tombstones by the bay
Ground, where generations lay.
Black umbrellas stacked to pray.
Pat's ashes held for such a day.
My clutched fingers opened as they may,
And the wind took me "Da" away.

The evening before we departed from Ireland, Barbara and I, with Aunt Anne Marie and husband Karl Nygren, co-hosted a farewell family dinner. We planned the gathering at Danny Minnie's Restaurant for Aunt Susie, Sheila McFadden (cousin), her husband Hughie, Uncle Eddie O'Donnell, her partner Frances Sharkey, and others.

Danny Minnie's, a unique country place, had a surprising level of elegance for rural Ireland, upon arrival pre-dinner drinks were served fireside. From there, one moved to the dining room, which was magnificently filled with tall fresh flowers. The evening was replete with delicious food, shared stories and poems. It made it easy to understand why the Irish don't forget anything, even across generations, including tales of tragedy, sadness, and joy.

The restaurant, filled with patrons as well as a special group of travel writers, echoed boisterous good humor. Our dinner drew to a close, and one of our guests, Hughie McFadden, asked if he might sing a song as a farewell tribute. We were all thrilled. Hughie stood at the end of the table and, in an ancient, warbly, pure-pitched tenor voice, sang "Danny Boy." The restaurant suddenly went quiet. No one moved. The staff froze, full of emotional pride like a national anthem. Hughie's voice ached with love and loss. When he ended, there wasn't a dry eye in the place, and no one wanted the moment to end. Suddenly, wiping their eyes, thunderous applause erupted with hearty bravos and yelps of appreciation. It was a proper Irish send-off no one will ever forget.

I was beginning to feel I never wanted to leave. My friend Jeremiah Durick once wrote, "Despite the rain and dampness which creeps into the bones. It wasn't a total surprise the early Irish worshipped the sun while their lungs weakened, potatoes rotted in the field, and everything stayed green. After days of drizzle, fog, and rain, shoes get heavy, clothes never dry, and a dismal feeling can emerge. On such a day, it would be easy to find locals sitting in a pub, buying another 'round' and hoping the tales and storytelling never end."

Too soon, it was time to say goodbye. Aunt Susie smiled and expressed her hope, "Through the years, I've witnessed a number of families returning to Ireland to see mothers, fathers, and families from the 'old sod.' There's always hugs and handshakes with the admonition, 'You can always come back, you're welcome,' and I say the same to you today!" She quickly added an old Irish proverb: "When the fun is at its height, it's time to go." There were warm embraces and tears. Everyone knew they might not see each other again. It was easy to think of how many tearful departures happened at the same historic family cottage.

On our journey home, messages from my brothers came pouring in about the short poem I'd written for Pat's burial.

Kevin was the first to respond: "Da is one with the man in the wind and the west moon. He shall have stars at elbow and feet."

Rich penned, "Dad is where he wished to be laid to rest. He wanted Mom to join him there, but she demurred. As his oldest son, you have done him a great service, and I am eternally grateful. I am so moved you and Pat's baby sister, Anne Marie, were there to return his essence to the soil of our ancestors. In time, I hope to follow your steps and pilgrim to the stone in the cemetery and feel the wind."

Terry added, "Your words from the craggy slate-filled green hills of Burtonport were sparse as the land is moving. You did a wonderful thing to take Pat back and release him there in the wild and tamed countryside and all, with his older family and relations circling around above and below as they tend to do in West Donegal. It's the wind, you know. The wind, and sea; it's all quite unlike anywhere else on earth, so far away from it all, there exposed to nature's breath."

~ 22 ~

THE FIFTH AVENUE GIRL

While in Ireland, we received news from Rita that her husband, Eddie, had suddenly died.

"He was sitting at the kitchen table, keeled over, and fell to the floor." She described being in absolute shock and dismay at what had happened and what to do. She rushed to revive him. She thought he might have had a stroke or a heart attack. Trying to move him was impossible; he was too heavy. She ran to the phone and called 9-1-1. Within minutes, the EMTs arrived. They were too late. There was nothing they could do. Rita felt desperate, worthless, emotionally distraught, and lost. What would she do now?

Upon our return from Ireland, we rushed to Rita's side and tried our best to console her. Part of the tragedy was that it was so unexpected. It would take some time to reconcile. A memorial service for Eddie was planned for the summer. A local event for family and friends would be held at his favorite Rutland restaurant. Aside from Rita, Barbara and I welcomed a friendly group of neighbors who reflected upon their affection for Eddie, all mentioning his well-known sense of humor. I prepared a thoughtful tribute with sentimental and humorous reflections to honor him for my mother, Rita.

Rita had done her best. She said her goodbyes and carefully planned the memorial event with a characteristic eye for detail and dramatic flair. Now, she had to go home, adjust to being alone, and make a new life for herself. Although we were only two hours away, for Rita, it felt like a million miles.

Some days after Eddie's memorial service, I shared with Rita all the details about bringing Pat's ashes to Ireland. She listened intently and said, "I remember when I first heard the news that Pat died. I could feel my face go flush as the tears flowed. I couldn't help thinking about what might have or could have been."

***

Now, Rita faced her own end-of-life journey. When my grandmother, Ethyl, died at ninety-four, she was completely blind. Rita began her own struggle with diminished vision, which meant she could no longer drive a car. She had faked her ability to do so for years. Finally, her ophthalmologist delivered the bad news, "No more driving." Grudgingly, she accepted her fate. It was a tough year as Rita adjusted to being alone. Despite seeing her as often as we could, the tragic day came when I received a call from the Rutland Medical Center. Rita had admitted herself with serious digestive tract bleeding. She had a lifelong battle with acid reflux, heartburn, and other related digestive maladies. The hospital determined her digestive tract had reached its limits, and surgery was required to repair a variety of long-neglected issues. The most serious was a hole in her diaphragm, allowing part of her stomach to constrict her left lung.

Once again, we were outside the country when we were alerted to Rita's predicament. I immediately made plans to fly to the U.S. to be with her. Rita's half-sister, Terry, who was living in Tennessee at that time, and niece, Kelly, joined me for the bedside vigil. The surgery was successful, but Rita's recovery seemed uncharacteristically slow; she lacked motivation and had let go of her 'pick yourself up, dust yourself off' dramatic nature.

I spoke with Rita's surgeon: "Doctor, when I look at my mother, she doesn't appear robust. I know she is fresh from surgery, but her condition appears more than just a little fragile. To me, she looks like she could die. Is this my imagination?"

The doctor empathetically suggested, "Yes, it's a good possibility, but living is up to your mother. I've done the best I can. The question is, does she want to live? In rehab, she might rebound and get her strength back, but at her age, it will be a challenge. The future is in her hands."

Within a few days, Rita was transported to a nearby Rutland rehab facility to convalesce and regain her mobility. She put on her game face, but when challenged to participate in rehabilitation, Rita feigned disinterest in regaining her mobility. This was a critical point in her general well-being. If she couldn't walk, she couldn't go home. It was her moment to live with the choice she made. Despite the encouragement, Rita dismissed exercise as being as useless as water.

Soon, Rita was moved to a different wing of the rehab center. She increasingly exhibited cognitive dissonance. The staff recommended she be moved to the Memory Care unit, where she received assistance. At eighty-eight, her inactivity, surgery, and age slowed her down.

Barbara and I visited Rita often over the next two years. This made us acutely aware of her deterioration. She spent our time together touching things, her gown, her sheets, her face, and her hair, as if she knew life was ending and she needed to feel everything one last time. Shortly, after her 90th birthday, Rita died on August 12, 2017. We were with her till the end.

She was cremated and interred next to her husband, Eddie, at Rutland's Tennybrook Cemetery. As Rita requested, the burial was a private service with just us, the funeral director, her ashes, and a Catholic priest. A celebration of her life was planned for the fall with family and friends.

Rita's Christmas card list served us well in our efforts to make sure her extended family and a lifetime of friends knew of her passing. They were all invited to come to Rutland to help celebrate her life. Obituaries were placed in multiple newspapers in Vermont and New York State, where her brother George's family lived. We held Rita's memorial service on October 10th at the Red Clover Inn. It was a spectacular fall day. The peak of color warmed us all. The ceremony took place in a small red barn adorned with festive lights coiled around wooden beams. Endless entertaining vignettes of "Rita's Life" were told to everyone's delight.

I stood to deliver a eulogy for Rita and briefly tell her story. This helped launch other recollections, humorous stories, and words of love:

"Good morning! Welcome, one and all, family and friends, to the life celebration of Rita June Boomhower Mills. I am Rita's son, Michael. Rita's best-kept secret for forty-five years! Thank you all so much for coming today to help celebrate 'Rita...Rita...Rita!'

"We are grateful to those who have traveled long distances and at considerable expense to be here. I especially want to recognize my dear cousins (the Leddy's) from Burlington, Vermont who are in attendance here today. They are much-beloved cousins and family of my mother, who adopted me. They never met Rita. I wish to thank all those who visited Rita during the past year and a half, telephoned, sent cards, and took care of her (some of Rita's wonderful caregivers are here with us). I especially want to thank my brother Rich and wife El, who were the only ones to ever know Rita. It is important to mention that the beautiful flowers here in the barn are from Rita's niece, Cheryl O'Brien, her husband, Dave, and their daughter, Ally, who could not be with us. If Rita could be here, she would have been so pleased to see each of you. Rita would say she was 'all nerved up' with excitement and needed a 'scotch and soda.'

"We would like to begin our remembrances with Rita's family: the Wilson/Lucks, Robinsons, and Stapchuks, and then open it up to *any and all* who wish to participate in a vocal way.

"Before we start, I would like to introduce my family, Rita's legacy. Please stand for a moment when I mention your name: my wonderful wife of forty years, Barbara Wilson; Rita's grandsons,

Jonathan and Sean; Rita's granddaughter, Holly; Sean's two children as well as Rita's great grandchildren, Patrick and Kathryn (Katie) Luck.

"Today is the closing of Rita's long-running Broadway play of life. Imagine, while we were standing in line waiting to get into the theatre, Rita stepped over the soft velvet rope for our queue and snuck in first to save good seats for the rest of us.

"We all have mothers. We all lose them, although never in the same way. We stand at the edge of loss, attempting to retrieve some memory, some human meaning from the silence, something precious and gone. But to know Rita, you have to know a piece of Rita's life story which was a secret for so many years. At nineteen, she gave birth to me after a whirlwind romance with my birth father, Patrick Ward, at the family's summer resort in East Durham, New York. As the summer ended, Rita realized she was pregnant."

I then briefly shared the whole story as Rita would have done herself.

"Unfortunately, Rita never met my adoptive parents, Bill and Mary Luck, because my mother, Mary Leddy Luck, died before I found Rita. My adoptive father, Bill Luck, lived near us in an assisted care facility in El Paso, Texas, and then later in Massachusetts.

"Several years after finding Rita, I vividly remember driving our car and asking if she had any interest in seeing where my adoptive parents were buried. She said, 'Yes.'

"We made a small detour and drove to the Resurrection Park Cemetery in South Burlington, Vermont, so Rita could see the gravesite. She was about to get out of the car when she was overcome with sobbing and couldn't move. She was paralyzed. She never moved.

"Since then, I had imagined (with homage to my favorite Irish poet Billy Collins) when Rita gave birth to me, she might have whispered, 'Here is a gift of your breathing body, beating heart, strong legs, bones and teeth, and two clear eyes to read the world.'

"Now, I wish to give back to Rita a much smaller gift than she gave me: 'The archaic truth, you can never repay the woman who gave you your life." There have been times when I have foolishly thought just finding Rita and caring for her would be enough to make us even. It wasn't.

She was a genuine character, an original. She never in all the years I knew her played anyone's game, but her own. She was a woman of simple honor and courage. She determined at some point to live her life with substance, style, and character and she did her best with what she had.

Anyone in Rutland will attest that Rita was "The Fifth Avenue Girl" anywhere she went. She learned to be a champion seamstress and inherently knew how to make or alter quality clothes. She could easily remake a collar on a jacket turn just enough to create a perfect *Vogue* style.

Rita, "the perfectionist," took great pride in everything she did. This standard required exceptional talent, perseverance, and an indestructible zest for life. It was this quality that made her voice and her laughter infectious, vital, and unforgettable. Rita always was an unparalleled combination of fun and fury. She had an ability to turn on her spark and make her surroundings seem pale and wan.

No one loved a good joke more than Rita. She always tried to be funny. A few years ago, she told me, "I can't get my sweaters on over my head anymore, which I can't understand because the way my brain works, everything goes over my head." For entertainment, Rita named a squirrel who was exceptionally large and unsuccessful at raiding her bird feeder "Numb Nuts."

On Rita's ninetieth birthday, her sister, Terry, and niece, Kelly, joined us for an outdoor birthday party at her Mountain View Nursing Center. We all knew it was Rita's last birthday. With Veuve Clique champagne, we celebrated with chocolate cake lovingly made by Kelly, party hats, sparklers, and two breathtaking bouquets of flowers from her niece, Cheryl, and her family, as well as Rita's oldest grandson, Sean, and Rita's two great-grandchildren.

I always suspected Rita's life was like a five-card stud poker game. She was dealt five-cards with no chance to throw any away in exchange for new ones. She had to play the hand she was dealt, whether it was good, mediocre, or lousy. I'd like to think Rita played her hand well, she bluffed when she needed to, almost always bumped her bet and played her cards with conviction.

Now, Rita's life journey is over. She lived a life worthy of respect, filled with adventure, wisdom, laughter, love, and grace, and she did this all in the company of so many people who loved and admired her. We never lose anything good."

Barbara set a more humorous tone with stories about Rita:

"One day in a restaurant, Rita was returned from the ladies' room with a fresh face and knowing swagger. As she turned the corner on her way to our table, her coat belt caught the back of a seated gentleman's chair. Reluctant to notice the tug on her coat, she kept going. Before she knew it, she was unwittingly dragging the man behind her while he was still seated. I burst into laughter, along with a few others, who noticed the sequence of events. It was quite a spectacle! As she turned around, she saw a groundswell of applause. It was a recognition of a strong woman taking a man for a ride!! Not one to shun attention, Rita relished all the attention for as long as possible. At the right moment, she turned, looking shocked. In an astonished voice, she apologized to the much-bemused man, disentangling himself to return to his lunch. I think she loved every second of her unwitting performance and would probably do it again if she could have."

Rita's sendoff was a chance for many of Rita's "Dear Ones" to easily get to know each other, catch up on local news, and meet others who loved her. She always told us she "wanted to go out in a blaze of glory." She would have been pleased with the day. Barbara and I noted that the calendar date, October 10[th,] was the same as the date when we had scattered Pat's ashes at the Donegal family cemetery.

EPILOGUE

What had begun as one notion of being adopted, in the end, answered one of the most complicated of human needs: "Who am I?"

During my adoption journey I experienced so many joys as well as great sorrow. I played hard as a boy and grew into an adventuresome, independent adult. There were many lessons learned. I think my wonderful cousin, Jim Leddy, summed it up well at my mother's Life Celebration when he said, "I join with you today to now know Rita. I never met her. I knew her son, who today speaks of having two mothers. Who knew? Who knew? Just imagine the wonders of having two mothers who give of themselves to their children. The selfless, unconditional love of a woman who gave birth to you and the woman who nurtured your heart, mind, and soul, offering you to adulthood."

Cousin Jimmy was right. It was wonderous and moving to learn about others, how they thought and felt, reflecting on life's values and social norms. My greatest gift was the love received, given so caringly and made more precious by my bearing witness, like all of you, to happiness, forgiveness, and personal disappointments. I loved and buried my adoptive and birth parents. They both instilled in me strong feelings regarding how good people are and how so many touch the human spirit.

The search and discovery process was overwhelming and remarkably rewarding. I discovered within me a precious and valuable truth. Love is universal and must be carefully nurtured. I was a lucky one; I found everyone. There was no sense of failure. I was able to accept the frailties of suggested differences and discover tolerance and peace within myself. The stage was set, the characters' roles were full of life, and I appeared uninvited at a grand party, where one and all embraced me. I couldn't have asked for more.

Rita's decision to give me away for adoption left me with a family I needed and loved. Everyone wants to belong somewhere, and I belonged with them. So, this story of adoption and discovery has as much to do with time and place as it does with family characters; it was a stage for a deeper level of respect and understanding.

I understood Rita's favorite place was the Catskills, where her family resort was located close to her grandparent's home. I was able to visit the resort, which was past its prime, but I could still imagine the particulars of the place: a swimming pool and a well-groomed lawn where resort guests enjoyed the sunshine and trails leading to refreshing mountain waters. It was a home away from home where guests, year after year, spent endless hours enjoying delicious meals, chatting with family and friends, lots of music and dancing, and table and lawn games. This all reflected Rita's innate love of life and her well-developed sense of hospitality. The Catskills location has many similarities to a Hudson Valley School landscape painting, robustly focused on not only the beauty of nature but also tantalizing the senses with the pleasure of fresh air, a luxury for city dwellers. The Catskill location beckoned young and old to wander trails to secret falls, where stolen kisses awakened a sense of overall well-being.

Rita often interjected her excitement and pleasure, saying, "It's just like New York!" This saying became popular post-WWII, when young people were home again, stepping out and having fun in the city. As an accomplished seamstress and lifetime fashion queen, Rita's appearance was the beginning of a performance played out walking to the store for her mother or being noticed at the public pool. She was quite a character and always ready for a party. She brought with her quips and quotes, astutely memorized from her newspaper clippings, and a personal wit that beguiled everyone. I thought she was "the cat's whiskers," a phrase she would have approved.

Over the years, Barbara and I have enjoyed countless family occasions with Rita, particularly weddings, where we learned to appreciate that the fruit doesn't fall very far from the tree. Her family traditions were generously planned events in beautiful places with lots of music, drinks, and laughter to celebrate others and uplift the spirit. Everything was perfect. Rita and her family would have it no other way.

Rita's worldly goods found a place within her home. She took great pride in her home ownership, collections, the provenance of items, traditional order, and cleanliness. She lived up to the expectations in her social world. Her legacy rested in family letters from the Civil War, poetry she wrote to me in my absence, and mountains of music, movies, newspaper clippings, and books.

Similarly, my much shorter relationship with Patrick eventually resulted in a settled time together. He often postured or held court on topics in his comfort zone, and I learned from them. His stories were fascinating. The secret to being a new immigrant Irish family is that often one lives in poverty. Bayonne, New Jersey, was a bedrock of families of strong character, broken apart by war and environmental destruction; a location where hard-working poor worked in shipyards that were singularly backbreaking. There are heartbreaking stories of sweat and dirt intertwined with brooms sweeping clean wooden floors before simple meals for which one was eternally grateful. Intermittent moments of levity were filled with traditional music and dance enjoyed with a dash or more of spirits. The traditional twirl of a skirt and sense of belonging morphed naturally into a mythology of an Irish family's life and times.

Patrick's Irish family originated in Donegal, Ireland, where a small homestead rests securely close to the tides of the sea and the light of Gods, where leprechauns still light fires for the departed. These sensibilities remained deep in his soul, inspiring many of his lifetime transitions in place. Patrick's life was replete with interchangeable places, where he dedicated his enviable ability, earned through education and hard work. He was well versed in the art of blarney and was an able leader. His passion for stage performance infectiously inspired others to participate in various thrilling and "unique" productions at work and on stage.

Patrick's worldly goods were simple. They included carpets woven and created by tribesmen who met on ancient roads of Iran and traveled across by all walks of life. Ancient ceramic treasures were discovered buried in sand dunes close to his Iranian home, which later accompanied him to San Francisco. Symbolically, a piano, fine art, sculpture, and a legion of his wife, Donna's discoveries. These were his tangible legacy.

As an expat in Saudi Arabia, Iran, and Greece, he intuitively assimilated Persian and Greek cultural heroes into his expression, an inexplicable power of desert Gods reflected in Saudi Arabian and Iranian light and shadows. This inspiration touched his soul like glimmers from the seas of Donegal, Greece, San Francisco, and New York. He passed all this on to his sons. It was a perfect union with earthly and spiritual life.

Fortunately, I got the privilege of meeting and getting to know my birth mother, Rita, for twenty-five years and my father, Pat, for almost seven. Even with all that precious time, our lives were different, separate. Maybe the notion of a stranger being folded into another family is too much of a challenge to an adoptee's established sense of identity. The time and experiences that nurture who we think we are don't dissolve after 45 years of a singular understanding of self.

To me, it felt more like I was the one adopting my birth parents. We were graciously welcomed into their traditions and serenaded with stories from their past. We built memories together, only to have my parents leave me again. It seemed like an irretrievable sequence of serendipitous moments, an all too abrupt end to the story.

One thing I know for sure is that my children and grandchildren are the loves of my life. They are always present in my mind. My own misgivings about my choices, separation from my older children, and job demands, which limited even my time with my youngest son, were ameliorated in large part by my wives. They were both wonderful and loving mothers and partners.

Inherently, I know that if I have contributed any small good in my life, Bill and Mary Luck deserve overwhelming credit. They were my parents. They provided the grace of a loving home when I needed it the most. Along with my adopted siblings, Nancy and Rosemary, I will always be indebted to them. They were simply wonderful. It is clear each adopted child is a combination of both the adopted and birth parents. I cannot discard either nurture or nature; it is a mixture of both. The benefits I received as an adopted child were to be raised in a strong, loving family and in a community where I could grow and learn in safety, be young and foolish, and be forgiven for bending the rules. My adoptive parents were solid role models, demonstrating the value of education and hard work, and my birthparents provided the innate qualities that made me physically strong, stubborn, theatrical, adventuresome, and compassionate.

Perhaps, despite how hard we try, we all die unhealed, and love is the ultimate secret after everything else is gone.

Maybe I was lucky.

I got the best of both worlds.

Michael F. Luck, Ph.D. is a tried-and-true Vermonter, whose hard work and serendipity helped advance his career as a senior executive at universities and healthcare systems. A natural talent in theater arts, leadership, and teamwork paved the way to a successful professional life.

An Educational Anthropologist, Dr. Luck has a keen understanding of kinship systems, how genetics gives us our roadmap in life, and the way in which humor is used as a social lubricant.

Dr. Luck's philanthropic leadership raised more than $4.5 billion for the betterment of hospitals, colleges, universities, and civic organizations: MIT, Rutgers University, the 64 campuses of the State of New York (SUNY), Wayne State University-Detroit, Healtheast, University of Massachusetts Boston, and more. Underscoring his career, his book, "Community College Development: Alternative Fundraising Strategies" (R&R Newkirk, Inc.), was hailed as a national landmark study.

The great outdoors is where Michael is happiest: hiking, gardening, and exploring. International cuisine, discussion of history, film, theater, music, and museums enrich his well-being with an occasional scotch with good friends.

Michael has three children and two grandchildren. He and wife, Barbara C. Wilson, Ed.D. divide their time between Vermont and Spain.

Michael F. Luck

www.ingramcontent.com/pod-product-compliance
Lightning Source LLC
Chambersburg PA
CBHW070056080526
44586CB00013B/1076